DANCING

ARTS FOR HEALTH

Series Editor: Paul Crawford, Professor of Health Humanities, University of Nottingham, UK

The *Arts for Health* series offers a ground-breaking set of books that guide the general public, carers and healthcare providers on how different arts can help people stay healthy or improve their health and wellbeing.

Bringing together new information and resources underpinning the health humanities (that link health and social care disciplines with the arts and humanities), the books demonstrate the ways in which the arts offer people worldwide a kind of shadow health service – a non-clinical way to maintain or improve our health and wellbeing. The books are aimed at general readers along with interested arts practitioners seeking to explore the health benefits of their work, health and social care providers and clinicians wishing to learn about the application of the arts for health, educators in arts, health and social care and organisations, carers and individuals engaged in public health or generating healthier environments. These easy-to-read, engaging short books help readers understand the evidence about the value of arts for health and offer guidelines, case studies and resources to make use of these non-clinical routes to a better life.

Other Titles in the Series:

Reading	Philip Davis
Film	Steven Schlozman
Singing	Yoon Irons and Grenville Hancox
Theatre	Sydney Cheek-O'Donnell
Drawing	Curie Scott
Photography	Susan Hogan
Storytelling	Michael Wilson
Music	Eugene Beresin
Painting	Francisco Javier Saavedra-Macías, Samuel Arias-Sánchez, and Ana Rodríguez-Gómez
Magic	Richard Wiseman
Video	John Quin
Body Art	Brian Brown and Virginia Kuulei Berndt
History	Anna Greenwood
Creative Writing	Mark Pearson and Helen Foster
Games	Sandra Danilovic

DANCING

BY

NOYALE COLIN

London Contemporary Dance School, UK

And

KATHRYN STAMP

Coventry University, UK

emerald
PUBLISHING

United Kingdom – North America – Japan – India
Malaysia – China

Emerald Publishing Limited
Emerald Publishing, Floor 5, Northspring, 21–23 Wellington Street, Leeds LS1 4DL.

First edition 2025

British Library Cataloguing in Publication Data
A catalogue record for this book is available from the British Library

ISBN: 978-1-83753-915-4 (Print)
ISBN: 978-1-83753-912-3 (Online)
ISBN: 978-1-83753-914-7 (Epub)

INVESTOR IN PEOPLE

We should consider every day lost on which we have not danced at least once.

Friedrich Nietzsche
(1844–1900)

CONTENTS

LIST OF FIGURES

FOREWORD: CREATIVE PUBLIC HEALTH

The 'Arts for Health' series aims to provide key information on how different arts and humanities practices can support, or even transform, health and wellbeing. Each book introduces a particular creative activity or resource and outlines its place and value in society, the evidence for its use in advancing health and wellbeing and cases of how this works. In addition, each book provides useful links and suggestions to readers for following-up on these quick reads. We can think of this series as a kind of shadow health service – encouraging the use of the arts and humanities alongside all the other resources on offer to keep us fit and well.

Creative practices in the arts and humanities offer a fantastic, non-medical, but medically relevant way to improve the health and wellbeing of individuals, families and communities. Intuitively, we know just how important creative activities are in maintaining or recovering our best possible lives. For example, imagine that we woke up tomorrow to find that all music, books or films had to be destroyed, learn that singing, dancing or theatre had been outlawed or that galleries, museums and theatres had to close permanently; or, indeed, that every street had posters warning citizens of severe punishment for taking photographs, drawing or writing. How would we feel? What would happen to our bodies and minds? How would we survive? Unfortunately, we have seen this kind of removal of creative activities from human society before, and today, many people remain terribly restricted in artistic expression and consumption.

I hope that this series adds a practical resource to the public. I hope people buy these little books as gifts for family and friends, or for hard-pressed healthcare professionals, to encourage them to revisit or to consider a creative path to living well. I hope that creative public health makes for a brighter future.

Professor Paul Crawford

PREFACE

The arts have long been engaged in communities to support the vital work happening in a multitude of health settings, as a means of maintaining or improving health and wellbeing. Increasingly, dance has been put forward to offer solutions for social recovery through educational, community and social care projects. Dance has become a significant contributor to the therapeutic ethos permeating all facets of culture. Dance offers a unique approach to tackling health and wellbeing due to its dual identity as a physical activity and a creative form of expression. Whereas the experiential aspect of contemporary dance is particularly relevant to a therapeutic context, there are many other forms of dance that are supporting health.

Dance and movement are everywhere, in all different settings. Formalised dance delivery can take place in care homes, studio spaces, dance clubs, church halls and at home, to name only some. This volume will introduce a number of dance and movement styles that are used in community and health settings, including ballroom, ballet, modern and contemporary dance and Asian dance, as well as fitness-based forms such as Zumba. Many case studies come from the UK, but there are a number from elsewhere in the world, so some cultural and national dance forms are explored. While the primary focus is on amateur engagement with dance, the benefits of undertaking dance professionally and in formal training is explored through our evaluation of dance as an activity with therapeutic benefits.

There is a growing need for accessible, guided literature about how dance can advance health and wellbeing (Chappell et al., 2021). While physical activity is directly linked to health, dance has not always been associated with healthy practice. Safety and accessibility issues in dance have been at the centre of recent research that has contributed to new insights and recommendations for safe and inclusive dance practice for a wide range of participants in both professional and amateur contexts (Quin et al., 2015; Whatley et al., 2018). Less focus on physical aesthetics and virtuosity and more emphasis on the experience of the participants in dance have allowed a shift in the understanding of safe practice in dance. It is within this shifting landscape that the relationship between the physical, mental and social in dance has been more significantly applied to the treatment or support of a range of conditions. While increased participation is a welcomed, positive shift, dance must be delivered safely by facilitators who are trained/experienced. Dance activities for vulnerable people must be carefully managed to avoid harm and address issues of accessibility. For example, dance for people with dementia should be delivered with care and particular attention to what dance engagement could trigger, similar to dance movement psychotherapy as a therapeutic treatment option.

There are dance practitioners working across the globe, offering non-clinical but effective ways to maintain or improve physical and mental health and wellbeing. This volume documents, unpacks and recommends ways that individuals can utilise dance as a tool to manage aspects of their health and wellbeing. Written for both those new to dance and those well-experienced in it, *Dancing* gathers case studies from the UK and beyond that explore the ways in which dance is being utilised to tackle a range of health and wellbeing-related issues, including physical inactivity, Parkinson's and depression. This book is constructed as a guidebook for individuals to use, either solo or as part of a bigger group, with inspiration for guided activities that people can undertake, information on how to get involved in dance, case study examples to use as motivation to explore dance as a physical and creative activity. This guidebook approach, we hope, will equip you as readers with practical ideas for using dance and movement in developing bodily awareness, sense of self and engagement with others, key factors in maintaining healthy identities and improving social relationships.

ACKNOWLEDGEMENTS

Our first thanks must go to the organisations and individuals who serve as case studies in this book. Our mission with *Dancing* was to spotlight some of the brilliant, groundbreaking practice in dance and health spaces that, for many, is the result of years if not decades of experience. We thank you for your time and support in co-writing these small snippets of much bigger, nuanced practices. We hope we have captured something of the transformative work you do.

We are very grateful to the team at Emerald for their guidance and support in the development of the book. Special thanks goes to Katy Mathers and Prof Paul Crawford as fierce advocates for the message at the heart of this book series, and for supporting us in the maturing of our ideas through the proposal stages. Thanks also to Charlotte Maiorana and Pavithra Muthu for your guidance through the publication process.

This book was created through collaboration and many of the ideas flourished out of conversations we have had with colleagues and peers at certain events. Thank you to the attendees at the Dance for Health Research Network Day, held at the University of Winchester in June 2023. Thank you to Dr Emma Meehan and Dr Supritha Aithal for the time spent in conversation about the developing area of dance and health.

Thank you to colleagues at the Centre for Dance Research (C-DaRE) at Coventry University for their continued support in developing writing and cultivating a culture for dance research in which ideas can be challenged and nurtured. Similarly, we would like to thank colleagues at the University of Winchester and, in particular, Dr Catherine Seago for her stimulating contribution to this project. Funding received from University of Winchester and

Coventry University facilitated our collaboration and in-person co-writing sessions, which were invaluable, as well as helping to make this publication open access.

With continued thanks to our proofreaders Dr Tim Fletcher and Jonathan Stamp for always answering our call!

Above all, we are hugely indebted to all the dance participants who have shared (directly or indirectly) their personal experience of dancing and how it has transformed their health, wellbeing and overall, their lives. These testimonies have been the propulsion for writing the book and have cheered us along at times when we needed to just keep on dancing.

1

WHY DANCE? AN INTRODUCTION TO DANCING FOR HEALTH AND WELLBEING

Our first sensory awareness is through movement. Before being born, we dance through the movement of the breath, the movement of fluid and the creation of our own body. Movement precedes all other senses. On a collective level, dance predates language and has been part of human history since the earliest times. It brings embodied emotions to spiritual rituals and forges bonds within communities. Every culture has used dance as an integral part of life, whether it be to creatively tell a story, share a message or to celebrate.

Dance is a joyous and expressive art form that releases 'feel-good' hormones associated with increased feelings of happiness and confidence. Dancing offers all the benefits of physical activities with the added artistic benefit of creativity, self-expression and social connections. Dance participants engage in playful activities with the potential for transformation, discovery and cooperation. There is a substantial body of evidence of the effectiveness of dance practice in strengthening a person's resources and capacity for wellbeing. This is the position from where we will explore dancing for health and wellbeing through this book, but first, *what is dance?*

WHAT IS DANCE?

One of the first things you may have noted from our introductory paragraph is the use of the term 'movement' alongside 'dance' or 'dancing'. Historically, dance has been used as a non-verbal form of expression; to prepare for battle, as a form of protest, as an integral part of celebrations, rituals and as a form of social interaction (Grau, 1998). But dance can mean many things to different people, and there are also many preconceptions and misconceptions about what dance can be. In many cultures, dance is associated with celebration and performed collectively at significant events such as weddings, Bar Mitzvahs and New Year celebrations. Dancing can also be a symbol of national or cultural pride, through historic folk dance forms (Flamenco, Yoruba or Cossack), during events as a form of respect or intimidation (the Māori haka) or dancing taking place during national events, such as carnivals, sporting events or times of political change. Dancing and movement practices have also historically been used as a form of communication within oppressive environments where verbal communication was banned, such as African Gumboot dance, or as a form of self defence, such as Brazilian Capoeira.

For some people, dancing involves choreographed or learnt steps that are part of a codified dance style with a specific history and culture. This can include ballet, bharatanatyam, salsa, modern or contemporary dance and ballroom dance styles, to name a few. For others, dancing and moving is an exercise practice and can include activities such as choreographed aerobic classes or Zumba. Dancing does not have to be choreographed, but can be improvised or impulsive, such as dancing that takes place during rave events or creative dance workshops. Somatically based practices and mindfulness-informed activities such as yoga or Tai Chi are also movement practices that are very closely linked to dance practice. Dance is also used alongside other performing arts disciplines, such as music and drama, within musical theatre productions and utilised daily as a form of entertainment. You might frequent entertainment venues where you either observe dance, such as a theatre or cabaret venue, or participate in dance activity, such as a nightclub.

Dancing is both a physical and a creative practice, which makes it unique among arts and exercise practices. This dual identity means that both the practice of dance and the study of dance are broad. Some people might view dancers as athletes, others might see them as artists and many will identify as both. The multi-faceted nature of dance means that it is an ideal activity for developing, managing and sustaining one's health, both physical and mental. In addition, while dance can be performed alone, it is also a highly social practice that serves as entertainment and escapism on television shows and in films, for example.

The physical practice of dance shares some values and behaviours with more traditional modes of medical body rehabilitation, such as physiotherapy or physical therapy. However, the paradigm, lens or model through which movement is being conducted is the distinguishing factor.

> *For dance and for rehabilitation medicine, movement is both method and result. In the rehabilitation paradigm, movement is medicine. In the dance paradigm, movement is art. Often a single movement can be both. Perhaps, through this phenomenon of movement, the arts and medicine are more interdependent than we previously imagined. (Worthen-Chaudhari, 2011, p. 483)*

Interaction between medical practitioners and dance artists is growing, as many case studies in this book will highlight, bringing together different approaches to explore innovative ways to address public health concerns and inequalities.

DANCING FOR HEALTH

Similar to many of the books in this *Arts for Health* series, we approached this project with an expanded view of 'health and well-being', considering it not only in relation to medical understandings of health but also holistic approaches to living well. This includes considering the issues of health inequalities and what can impact them, how health can impact on quality of life measures such as education, work and relationships and how certain skills or traits are needed in order to advocate for your own health prospects.

There has been a growing eagerness to clarify approaches to arts and health, articulating the differences between those that are therapeutically rooted and those that are artistically rooted. Tensions have arisen over how different approaches value aspects of the practice in not only intention but also divergent methodology and delivery methods (Broderick, 2011). This is also true of the field of dance and health. Differences in approaches can be viewed in terms of primary and secondary intentions. Therapy-based practices employ art as a medium for encouraging expression and communication, with enjoyment of the art form seen as secondary, whereas dancers working in health contexts prioritise the experience of dance, with therapeutic and medical benefits being advantageous byproducts (Broderick, 2011).

While dance therapy and dance in health approaches both have their place and purpose, it needs to be made clear when and how these approaches are being employed. This is important not only for the participants to understand their care provision but also for the respective fields of health and dance to understand the lens through which dance activity is being delivered. We will be attempting to examine the instrumental or intrinsic value of dance (for/in health), which is needed (Blades, 2018, p. 11), while recognising the need to be cautious about exaggerating the value of dance, and acknowledging limitations and gaps that require more research (Clift et al., 2021).

The case studies presented in this book speak to the ways in which these approach-based tensions manifest themselves in practice, and how artists and practitioners have worked to address them. In the following sections of this chapter, we will present an overview of three approaches to the practice of dance and health that our case studies and discussions interact with, either resisting or embodying the values of these approaches: somatic-informed movement practice, dance as therapy and collaborative health.

SOMATIC-INFORMED MOVEMENT PRACTICE

Somatic-informed movement practice (SIMP) uses movement improvisation, sensory awareness, imagination and touch. While SIMP is not understood as a therapy as such, it offers therapeutic values which share some of the practical outcomes sought by the wider field of somatic practices, including an awareness of the presence of emotion, anatomy, affect, memory and dream and the regulatory support of the autonomic nervous system (Collinson, 2020).

In this book, we demonstrate how dance artists trained in SIMP help people recover a sense of wellbeing through applying their skills in supporting others to sense their bodies. Their abilities to observe the smallest shifts and changes in bodies enable a sense of movement to be expressed. While it might not look like dance in its conventional sense, it allows people to communicate through movements and the body. A focus on inner sensation and small internal movements relaxes and stimulates blood flow and provides participants with a healthier sense of wellbeing or even lessening of pain (Tufnell, 2017, p. 105).

Similar to mindfulness approaches, whereby awareness of the present moment can help relieve sensation of pain, the focus on the present moment in somatic dance is considered an effective way of managing pain.

> *The somatic dance practitioner can simultaneously support an increasing awareness of the whole body and of the environment outside of the body with the use of objects. The expertise of the dancer is the moving body and the ability to read and explore the potential for movement in others. The somatic dancer introduces these processes gently and in a person-centred way that is accessible to all. (Dowler, 2016, p. 24)*

In her research on SIMP in hospitals, Collinson shares a conversation with the dance artist Cai Tomos who reflects on his encounter with a patient who can't walk due to an infection in his leg.

> *P is very anxious and fearful of what the future might hold. I suggest that we do some work on the breath and the feeling of connection to his leg. I explain about the building of neural pathways through movement and encourage him to do what feels right. As we work together P begins to close his eyes and slowly move his leg a little. I asked him what it feels like, and he speaks of his leg being like a*

> *frozen lake. I gently ask if I can place my hand on or near his leg. The next 5 or 10 minutes are based on listening to P begin to describe and expand on his perception of his injured leg. I ask questions to encourage the dialogue. Slowly he begins to describe a thawing of this frozen lake and through this use of imagination and metaphor P's perception of his injury begins to broaden and with that his confidence. That afternoon P tells me he feels ready to work with the OT's [Occupational Therapists] to begin to try walking. I hear back from the OT that something has shifted from this session that allowed P the confidence to engage differently and perhaps with a little more confidence in his recovery. (Tomos in Collinson, 2020, p. 4)*

More detailed case studies of Arts and Health programmes using somatic dancers to support nurses and other caregivers as part of a multi-disciplinary team are outlined in Chapter 5. You will come to see that the notion of dance practice not intended as a therapy but having therapeutic benefits is a feature of many of the practices we explore and spotlight in this book. However, we recognise the place and value of dance as a therapy in its own right, so will explore this field briefly now.

DANCE AS THERAPY

Dance movement therapy (DMT) and psychotherapy (DMP) is a process that uses dance and movement within a therapeutic process to delve deeper into explorations using a psychosomatic approach. It works as a form of somatic therapy for dealing with mental health issues, trauma processing and information processing, for children and adults of all ages and abilities. 'DMP is an empathic creative process practised as individual and group therapy in clinical, community, and educational settings, as well as in private practice' (ADMP UK, 2024).

DMT places the emphasis on the emotional, cognitive, physical and social integration of a person by means of movement and dance. Trained therapists use movement to achieve a therapeutic aim which is at the heart of the intervention. This distinguishes

DMT from dance for health practices whereby therapeutic outcomes might be possible but are not the focus. Being exposed to creative movement might create a therapeutic value, but it happened as an additional result to the sense of wellbeing that dancing provides. DMT's process may not be pleasurable for the client, for therapy is not a recreational activity. It can be a demanding, and at times emotionally draining experience (Karkou & Sanderson, 2000). The inclusion of the term 'psychotherapy' in DMT can also be interpreted as an effort to establish the practice as a form of psychotherapy.

Although more research is needed to verify the high level of variability of findings, studies have evidenced that both DMT and dance interventions have persistent long-term effects by improving clinical, cognitive and psycho-motor outcomes (Koch et al., 2019).

COLLABORATIVE HEALTH

Among the body of evidence that advocates for quality of relationship in health care, the development of a strong therapeutic relationship has been found to be one of the key factors for positive experience and outcome in rehabilitation based on physical activities and exercises. Physical therapy studies have concluded that 'the clinical context that an exercise program is delivered within may be just as important as the exercise program itself' (Powell et al., 2023, p. 1). Building relationships that are based on equal and collaborative exchanges – with opportunities for negotiation and choices – enhances patients' engagement and recovery (Ocloo et al., 2020). In addition, collaboration among healthcare professionals to share knowledge and skills has led to more inclusive perspectives in health care. The term 'collaborative health' covers a number of related and overlapping concepts, including integrated care (NHS, 2014) or relationship-based care (RCGP, 2021), which recognise the value of the exchanges among clinical care teams and between caregivers and patients.

Dance artists working in health contexts and, in particular, practitioners who use somatic approaches describe the relational aspect of the process with their participants as 'co-creative'. They see co-creative practice as an emergent process – fluid, spontaneous and underlined by trust (Tufnell, 2017, p. 95). This emphasis on co-creation features in many of the case studies that we will present throughout this book, recognising the importance of developing agency and empowering people to advocate for their health needs, in spaces and at times where it is often challenging to do so.

DANCE ON PRESCRIPTION

Social prescribing schemes offer dance to people as a way to support their health and wellbeing. Sometimes referred to as community referral, they aim to connect people to activities and services, while breaking down access barriers to community-based care such as financial cost, distance and mental trepidation. Dance is one of the activities people can be socially prescribed, along with crafting, cooking and sports, and these sessions are often delivered within the community.

The National Academy for Social Prescribing refers to social prescribing as 'evidence based interventions, which are designed to improve health and wellbeing outcomes, by referring individuals to non-clinical services and activities typically offered by the local voluntary and community sectors' (Khan et al., 2023, p. 4). There is a growing body of evidence to support the implementation of social prescription, but it requires a great deal of partner networking and liaison. Building partnership with delivering organisations such as Aesop (Arts Enterprise with a Social Purpose) or Dance Network Association (see case study in Chapter 6). Social prescribing is a growing area of health and arts activity around the globe and has much potential to support and alleviate the pressures of traditional medical systems, but research into the impact and benefits of arts and social prescription needs more long-term investment. At the time of writing, international reports have mapped the global developments in social prescribing across 27 different health system contexts, including England, Scotland, Wales, Northern Ireland, Republic of Ireland, Canada, the United States, Portugal, Spain, the Netherlands, Finland, Italy, Germany, Austria, Poland, India, Iran, Japan, Singapore, Malaysia, China, Taiwan, South Korea, and Australia (Khan et al., 2023).

HOW TO ENGAGE WITH THIS BOOK

This book situates lived experience as core to engagement in dancing for health, for the self, for the healthcare practitioner and for the dance artist. In this same vein, we invite you to consider your own experience of dancing and use it to lead you through the book. Why have you picked up this book? What do you want to ponder about dancing for health? How do you want to engage with this practice? We encourage you to experience the book as you need to. This could be by reading from beginning to end or by selecting chapters that might be more relevant for you in the present moment. You may want to move in response to what you read, experiencing the process of making meaning through embodied practice.

As authors, both of us have engaged with the field of dance and health in different ways which complement each other's knowledge and experience. Noyale has been interested in the therapeutic value of dance as a way of combining her dance practice with her interest in other forms of bodywork and somatic practices such as yoga, shiatsu and, more recently, craniosacral therapy. Some of the exercises in this book have been inspired by Noyale's training in movement improvisation and her growing practice in fall prevention and healthy ageing. Kathryn's interest in dance and health is preoccupied with how health intersects with areas of societal provision, such as social justice, inclusion and education. In addressing these, she is eager to uncover more about tensions and issues such as the perception of health interventions as therapy and equitable access to health care through education and community provision.

This book is informed by dance for health research, but it is not written from the perspective of dance scientists. We have sought to present a collection of practices which offer a range of contemporary voices and methods that we have identified as making a contribution to the development of dancing in the field of arts for health.

On the one hand, we refer to longstanding practices and established organisations that have led the field of dance for health. On the other hand, we also present practices which are more 'under the radar', but which are making headway in addressing key challenges that relate to dancing in relation to difference, access and inclusion. We also spotlight work that engages with developing technologies and how dancing for health can utilise digital tools (see CoDa's case study in Chapter 6). Dance will always have emphasis on the moving body, which makes it an important artform for resisting the dominance of technology as replacement of the human body.

The practical aspects of the book are aimed more at the more novice, as professionals who already use dance in their practice will have already navigated some of the practical considerations outlined in these chapters. Nonetheless, we hope to have provided professional dancers with a range of ideas and insights to help them to further develop their own practice.

Likewise, although more of our focus as UK-based researchers is on local examples and reference to case studies involving the NHS, we draw in this work on a range of international examples running from Australia to Cambodia and from Brazil to the United States. We anticipate that all the country-specific examples we refer to will be of interest and relevance to a diverse international audience. Some qualifications in this respect are important to keep in mind, and we wanted to add a note here about language use.

Health is not only very personal but is also described in different ways within different contexts. These sometimes contradictory and sometimes overlapping contexts can be geographical, because different countries have diverse health services, but can also be discipline- and practice-specific. How medical and care professionals might discuss their work and the people they interact with will differ from how dance artists describe their practice and those they work with. The personal dimension of health also means that people will speak about their health and how it impacts on them in personal ways. In this book, we have attempted to remain truthful to the language of the practice, discipline and culture in the case studies. Therefore, there may be differences in language across the case studies, but this reflects how health and arts for health are not monolithic, but highly nuanced.

Throughout this introductory chapter, we have sought to explore what dance is and how dancing is used in different contexts and cultures, before introducing three approaches to dance and health practice that help to contextualise some of the discussions in the following chapters of the book. We provided an overview of how you might like to engage with the rest of the book, and of particular nuances of our approach that are important to keep in mind as you continue. Next, we will be delving further into the benefits and value of dancing for health.

2

WHAT HELPS? THE VALUE OF DANCING FOR HEALTH AND WELLBEING

This chapter offers an overview of the evidence for the value of dance activity in relation to health care, health and wellbeing. Continuing on from the introduction to dancing in the previous chapter, we will now explore the impact and experience of dancing for four key areas: mental health and wellbeing, physical health, communication and entertainment or escapism. In this chapter, we introduce the first case studies of the book, which act as real-world examples of the ideas and themes we are exploring, in action.

DANCE PROMOTES MENTAL HEALTH AND WELLBEING

There is a strong body of evidence suggesting a link between dance and mental wellbeing. Engaging in dance-based activities can have a positive impact on many different aspects of wellbeing including overcoming depression and learning disabilities. Creativity develops people's sense of identity and self-efficacy and increases resilience, which is a key component of good mental health especially for young people (Catterall & Peppler, 2007). The act of participating in the arts lowers cortisol levels in the bloodstream (lowers stress) (Kreutz et al., 2004). Studies have demonstrated that depression scores can reduce significantly after dance interventions (Akandere & Demir, 2011), which are more efficient at improving mental health than other physical activity (Kim & Kim, 2007). Dance can also make a positive impact on future aspirations (Potter et al., 2015 in Mansfield et al., 2018).

Many studies have demonstrated the value of dance activity for key conditions such as anxiety, stress, mood, depression, memory, dementia, language development and attention. Feelings of self-confidence and self-esteem have been found to increase through dance participation (Christensen & Chang, 2021) and dance sessions have been described as a time-out from daily stress. Being able to express emotion through movement has been viewed as a source of stress reduction (Duberg et al., 2016; Hanna, 2017), with the physicality of dance aiding elevation of mood and relieving anxiety (Froggett & Little, 2012). Dancing can have positive benefits for social integration, and be a means of self-discovery, increasing one's sense of worth (Mansfield et al., 2018).

For young people, dance has been recognised as an intervention that can have positive impacts on their psychosocial health and wellbeing, including reduced reliance on mobile devices and increased confidence (Archbold & Bond, 2020). We can receive the benefits of dance across key life stages, with dancing also contributing to healthy ageing. The integrated activation of physical, cognitive and social skills promoted by dance has a positive effect on older people's life satisfaction (Cruz-Ferreira et al., 2015) and can be an important way to contribute to healthy ageing. A major side effect of dancing is that we just feel better afterwards! Dancing can enhance wellbeing at all ages.

DANCE PROMOTES COGNITIVE PROCESSES

Dancing incorporates the cognitive processes of learning steps and remembering choreographic sequences. Dance and choreography have been associated with a range of cognitive functions, including attention, imagery, problem-solving and short- and long-term memory (Stevens & McKechnie, 2005). The exercise of repetition and rehearsal when dancing improves mental dexterity (Hackney & Bennett, 2014), and the embodied thinking involved in dancing helps the brain find new ways of thinking and creates new neural circuits (Lovatt, 2020). Learning through movement helps people absorb ideas better and improves their ability to retain information (Swift, 2017).

In the last decade, technological developments have allowed scientists to gather data on the brains of dancing bodies. Recent scientific hypotheses have posited that dance might enhance the function of the brain in two ways. Firstly, it might have the potential to improve internal brain connectivity by increasing 'the speed of conductivity, which could enhance the brain's ability to communicate information between different brain regions or networks' (Basso et al., 2021, p. 15). Secondly, dancing with a partner or as part of a group could improve the neurological synchronicity of communication between people. Following this, thinking processes can be redefined not just as an individual processes but as a shared experience that we can positively influence by dancing together (Basso et al., 2021).

These evidenced characteristics reveal the potential of dance to be used as a treatment for managing neurodegenerative disease. Clinical applications have been studied for neurological disorders such as autism spectrum disorder (ASD) and Parkinson's disease (PD). The potential for dance to develop physical synchronisation, sense of rhythm, and social reciprocity has driven studies to conclude that 'a dance intervention with an emphasis on mimicry may activate the "dormant" mirror neuron system in individuals with ASD' (Ramachandran & Seckel, 2011). Similarly, recent work in elderly adults has found that dance enhances prefrontal cortex-dependent executive functioning in areas including planning, working memory and cognitive flexibility (Basso et al., 2021). Studies have suggested that dancing can be a valid approach to slow down the natural age-related cognitive decline (Noguera et al., 2020).

Dance offers individuals suffering with dementia a practical strategy to form significant relationships using movement as the medium of interaction while experiencing both physiological and psychological benefits from dance participation (Ho et al., 2020). As a social activity, dance provides rhythmicity, motor coordination, balance and memory enhancement (Tao et al., 2021) while delivering all the benefits of a physical activity. Self-expression through dance can help dementia-related issues by enhancing cognitive function, reducing agitation and aggression and increasing the quantity and quality of social interactions of people living with dementia (Motta-Ochoa et al., 2021).

DANCE FOR PARKINSON'S: EXPERIENCE IN THE SOUTH OF BRAZIL[1]

Dança & Parkinson, Brazil

PD, a progressive neurodegenerative disorder, not only affects physical mobility but also has significant psychological and emotional impacts on people with PD. Recognising the potential of dance as a non-pharmacological intervention for people with PD, the 'Dance for Parkinson's' research and community project, affiliated with the Centre for Aging and Movement (CREM), was created in 2016 at the School of Physical Education, Physiotherapy and Dance (ESEFID), Federal University of Rio Grande do Sul (UFRGS), Brazil.

The project, led by an Associate Professor in Dance, involves active collaboration among undergraduate and postgraduate students from the arts and health area, such as artists, researchers/ academics and healthcare professionals. With a nine-year history, the project has been promoting Brazilian Dance sessions to provide improvements in the quality of life of people with Parkinson's. Over these years, a total of 80 people with clinical diagnosis of Parkinson's, aged between 40 and 84 years, of both sexes, from diverse ethnic backgrounds and across various socio-economic levels, were involved in the project (60% women, 40% men; 52% white, 48% black and mixed race).

The values that underpin the project are inclusivity, with the understanding that each participant brings a unique set of challenges and strengths, and respect for individual abilities and limitations, fostering a non-judgemental and supportive environment. Furthermore, the programme promotes empowerment, encouraging participants to embrace their bodies and abilities, irrespective of the physical constraints imposed by PD. The value of creativity is woven into every session, providing an avenue for self-expression and personal discovery.

Led by trained dance instructors, the Brazilian Dance sessions take place twice a week in a dance room at the ESEFID/UFRGS, and last one hour. The dance sessions are divided into four parts (Fig. 1): Part 1 – each participant is sitting on a chair, and the session begins with a warm-up and joint mobility exercise, gradually transitioning into more dynamic and rhythmic movements, working the torso and upper and lower limbs; Part 2 – standing with the support of a chair or ballet barre, participants undertake lower limb strength, balance and weight bearing exercises and ballet-based exercises using Brazilian songs; Part 3 – free-standing activities and improvisation including: moving around the room inspired by Brazilian social and folk dances, exploring the movements in the rhythm of the music, moving in different directions and at different space levels, exploring creativity and imagination, dancing in pairs; and Part 4 – cool-down including breathing exercises, joint mobility and upper and lower body stretching exercises.

The 'Dance for Parkinson's' project has proven to be a beacon of hope and resilience for its participants. The project underscores

Fig. 1. Brazilian Dance Sessions Format.

the potential for Brazilian Dance not only to enhance physical well-being but also to foster emotional resilience and create a sense of community among people facing a neurological disease.

A comprehensive assessment of the programme's impact reveals tangible benefits for the participants. Physically, the participants reported improved functional mobility, increased range of motion and enhanced balance. Emotionally and socially, the impact was equally relevant. The participants expressed a heightened sense of self-esteem, reduced feelings of isolation and the establishment of a strong support network within the dance community, improving their self-perceived quality of life. The project's success was further exemplified by the consistent attendance and the emergence of an enthusiastic cohort that eagerly anticipated each session.

A key strength of the programme lies in the testimonials of its participants, highlighting the impact on their lives. One of the participants, in her late 60s, shared: 'Dance for Parkinson's project has been a lifeline for me. It's not just about the physical movements; it's about rediscovering joy and reclaiming a sense of self that Parkinson's often takes away'.

Another participant reflected on the emotional dimension of the programme, stating: 'In the dance sessions, I feel a sense of freedom that goes beyond the physical limitations imposed by Parkinson's. It's like breaking free from the chains of the disease, if only for a moment'.

This case study demonstrates the beneficial impact of dance activity for people with a specific medical condition that attends to physical, emotional, mental and social needs, while also engaging with dance as a form of cultural celebration.

DANCE ENHANCES PHYSICAL HEALTH

The positive link between movement-based activity and health has been known for over 2,000 years (Walker, 2021). Regular physical activity has been shown to reduce the risk of coronary heart disease, diabetes and depression. It plays a key role, as the principal determinant in energy expenditure, in preventing obesity (WHO, 2024). Studies in dance have been shown to reduce BMI, increase cardiovascular fitness and improve bone health (Burkhardt & Brennan, 2012). As dance is a physical activity and engages the whole body, it is widely recognised as an important source of exercise. In particular, it has been evidenced that dance can enhance body composition, blood biochemistry (Lopez-Nieves & Jakobsche, 2022) and the musculoskeletal system.

Chronic pain is considered to be a global public health priority (Goldberg & Mcgee, 2011). New approaches are required to support the millions of people worldwide living with chronic pain. The Somatic Practice and Chronic Pain Network (UK), co-led by Dr Emma Meehan from Coventry University and Professor Bernie Carter from Edge Hill University, investigated the value of dance and movement for people living in pain and for healthcare professionals. Findings of the research have highlighted the benefits of methods which focus on subjective and experiential features. Somatic dance practice offers ways to modulate the 'sensation, emotion and environments associated with pain' (Meehan & Carter, 2021, p. 8). One of the key aspects of this method is the development of an enhanced sense of agency as the patient is encouraged to collaborate in a recovery process which promotes wellbeing. The network has produced resources to help understand its potential for helping people living with chronic pain in their everyday life as well as in the healthcare system, workplaces and public spaces (see further information in the resource section).

Studies have investigated the potential for dance interventions instead of existing rehabilitation or treatment programmes, including in the case of chronic respiratory disease, a leading cause of global morbidity and mortality (Philip et al., 2020) and chronic heart failure (Neto et al., 2014). The British Heart Foundation (n.d.) has also offered six key reasons why dance is good for heart health. In addition, recent studies have found that dance can have a significant reduction in falls and fear of falls among older people, due to its development of balance, agility and bodily control, in addition to increased confidence (Talker News, 2022). Thus, dance has the potential to save the NHS millions by preventing falls and providing rehabilitation activities when falls occur (Aesop, 2020, p. 24).

DANCE AND FALLS PREVENTION

The projected number of people living in older age in 2045 is almost double the current number. The section of this population that is more likely to suffer falls (people aged 80 and over) is growing the fastest. Its number is expected to triple in the next 30 years (WHO, 2022). Physical activity has a crucial role in preserving function and can be instrumental in supporting healthy ageing. However, contemporary society has seen an increase in sedentary behaviour, due to, for example, shifts in labour and the impact of transport and technology advances. The Sport England Active Lives survey shows that 25% of all adults are physically inactive but inactivity levels increase significantly as people age (Sport England, 2023). It is never too late to engage in physical fitness and to enjoy a more active and independent life. The principle of 'use it or lose it' is a good reference to describe what is happening to our bodies when we are sedentary. Immobilisations such as bed rest or seating for a prolonged period lead to active loss of bone and muscle. Research on fall prevention has revealed compelling findings about the relationship between inactivity and loss of independence in older age. One week in bed reduces strength by around 20%. Inactivity worsens once people cannot live independently any more. 80% to 90% of nursing home residents spend their time seated or lying which makes them weaker, more prone to fall and less likely to recover mobility once fallen. In 2000, among the 500 people admitted to hospital in the UK due to falls, 33 never went home (Skelton, 2010).

Evidence-based exercise programmes such as FaME or OTAGO are delivered by post structural instructors (PSIs) through the NHS, but, while people might make good progress to begin with, they rarely stick to the exercises post rehabilitation programmes (12 weeks) and, without continued practice, through time any improvements gained are lost (Aesop, 2020, p. 4). The barriers to sustained engagement among older adults were reported to be lack of discipline and motivation, poor physical health and caring responsibilities (Seppala & Velde, 2022, p. 3).

While successful fall prevention programmes remain challenging, evidence suggests that dancing reduces falls risk (Aesop, 2020; Blanco-Rambo et al., 2022). Demand for dance classes for older people in the UK is rising. Dancing offers fun and accessible, cost effective ways to engage in physical activity and can enable more people to maintain or improve their fitness and balance. Movement and dance classes for older people in community settings have a focus on developing physical skills that will prevent health conditions and accidents.

Hampshire County Council's Steady and Strong Dance Programme, UK

Steady and strong exercise programmes have been developed in community settings and leisure centres. Level 4 postural stability trained exercise instructors deliver over 90 classes a week across the county of Hampshire. In order to broaden the offer, expand the number of instructors and classes and increase the continuum of falls prevention classes, Hampshire County Council (HCC) is expanding its programme into dance-based activities. To do so, the scheme invested in training existing dance teachers in the region to develop a dance extension of the Otago falls prevention programme, which is currently under evaluation. This approach recognises that

> *Dance has a place in primary prevention of falls by helping older people maintain an active lifestyle in an activity they enjoy. Dance also has a place when people move on from specific targeted falls prevention programmes as we know that benefits gained in these may be lost if people do not remain active. (Later Life Training, 2023)*

Classes can be pre-booked with the qualified dance instructors at a relatively low cost for a dance class (below £10) or, in some cases, it can be accessed through doctors' referrals at a reduced cost for less than £5 (HCC, 2024).

The Steady and Strong Dance programme evaluation supported by HCC aimed to further understand what makes dancing improve ageing people's quality of life. Insights from the existing programmes have demonstrated that, while people might start steady and strong classes for falls-prevention benefits, often the reason they stay at classes long term is the fun and social aspect. While results of the intervention's evaluation are not yet available at the time of the publication of this book, observations from instructors and feedback from participants are revealing the significance of dance in fall prevention.

Dr Cathy Seago, who is leading one of the new steady and strong dance classes in Winchester, observes that participants enjoy moving fluidly together with others.

> *The Otago exercises which underpin the class sequences ensure a measured approach to increasing strength and improving balance while the dance sequences use rhythmic patterns and dynamic qualities to invite lively contrasts in the flow of movement direction and energy. Feedback shows that the participants are experiencing gains in their daily activities as well as really feeling the wellbeing benefits, through a growing confidence enabled by a holistic awareness of body-mind. (C. Seago, personal communication, 2024)*

This demonstrates and reinforces the idea that dance is a multifaceted activity that can address specific personal and public health concerns as well as engaging the whole person in managing their health and enjoyment.

DANCE AS A FORM OF COMMUNICATION AND SOCIAL CONNECTION

Dancing connects people together. It is a wordless form of communicating emotion. Dance requires no special equipment or apparatus – if you can move any part of the body, you can physically dance. Even simply viewing dancing can benefit people. Dance enables us to communicate through movement things that we cannot easily express verbally. This section will explore the ways in which dance can be used to help connect with others, not only as a communicative tool but as a social experience. In addition, this section will reflect on how connecting to others through dance increases social skills and can address issues such as loneliness and social isolation, which were particularly prominent during the COVID-19 pandemic.

Dancing bodies release sexual hormones such as endorphins, testosterone and oxytocin which trigger feelings of happiness and exhaustion. Biologists have posited the similarities of animal and human courtship rituals. Dances such as tango, salsa or merengue are certainly charged with attractiveness and seduction. For example, the tango has been proved to increase the level of the testosterone in both partners as a result of physical contact and shared movement (Quiroga et al., 2009). However, eroticism is only a byproduct and rarely the main motivation. In fact, studies have demonstrated that women's reasons for dancing are predominantly improving fitness, mental health and confidence or escapism (Christensen & Chang, 2021).

Our perception of dance is often informed by cultural stereotypes. For example, erotic dances such as belly dancing and pole dancing used to be considered spiritual events. Misunderstanding or ignorance of cultural differences in movement expression has led to misconceptions and the association of dance solely with sex. While some cultures and religions have banned dancing or controlled its practice, dancing can do much more as we have tried to demonstrate in this book.

As a non-verbal form of communication, dance can also provide a presentation mode that can connect people with different sensory, intellectual and access needs. Communicating public health messages is important in keeping society well. Just as it is used in advertisements, dance can be used to engage people in important discussions about health and share key health messaging. In 2016, Cambodia-based inclusive dance company Epic Arts partnered with WaterAid to create a series of videos that sought to communicate messages about water supply, sanitation and hygiene, specifically for marginalised groups who were most likely to be affected by lack of access to water. Communicating these messages had a positive knock on effect for public health. The partnership emerged after WaterAid found that the audiences they were trying to target would not read lengthy reports or instructions and so needed a new way to spark interest in the subject. A WaterAid staff member who had worked on the WASH campaign for 10 years believed that this approach to communicating ideas was the best they had experienced (Wicken, 2016). Finding engaging, visual and inclusive ways of communicating public health messages is important, and dance is an excellent option.

When we experience times of hardship with our health and wellbeing, those around are impacted too. They are the people who support us in our recovery, see us at our lowest and celebrate with us when we feel good. There is increasing evidence that demonstrates the importance and value of dancing *with* family members and caregivers as a way of connecting or reconnecting with them through a bodily movement practice (Parmar et al., 2022; Petts & Urmston, 2022; Whiteside, 2020). This can help repair relationships that have entered a new phase, democratise power relationships for a brief period and allow people to connect emotionally and physically in a way that goes beyond functional or medical interaction. The following case study explores the importance of group connection and creativity for those living with dementia and their caregivers.

THE INHERENT VALUE OF CONNECTING THROUGH DANCE COMMUNITY

Stories in the Moment®, USA

Stories in the Moment® is a programme for people living with dementia that uses dance and movement coupled with imagination and creativity to tell people's stories, enhancing modes of expression and communication (Fig. 2). This co-creative dance programme was developed with the initial intention to work alongside people who are living with dementia and use dance as a form of storytelling. It uses dance, as well as sound, music, imagery, touch and imagination, as a way to support the participants' (and their care partners') own sense of community. It recognises the multiple levels of marginalisation and stigma those living with dementia experience. *Stories in the Moment®* aims to break down expectations or limitations placed on communities of people living with dementia and de-silo the environments they are welcomed into.

Source: Photographer: Nuria Rius.

Fig. 2. Participants in *Stories in the Moment*® at Queens Community House Social Adult Day Services Programme in Forest Hills, NY, USA.

Each *Stories in the Moment*® class begins with a ritual Hello Body Dance, by saying hello and welcoming one another into the shared space. By engaging in this way, the group sets the container for their shared practice. Each time this practice is repeated, the group anchors themselves into a shared space of belonging and they build, moment by moment, movement by movement, the foundation of the community.[2]

> *Dance is an inherent part of our expression, and we all have the ability and should have the access to be able to participate and develop that if we wish. And that as a result, we have an opportunity to create and cultivate a stronger sense of belonging. We all possess the ability to hone our tools of being in community and with one another. By participating in co-creative dance, we also benefit and support our brain health and physical health. But I see these as secondary to these other components of strengthening tools of connection, agency and being in community. (M. Kaczmarska, personal communication, 2024, Stories in the Moment® Founder, 2024)*

The *Stories in the Moment*® programme, as with many organisations/initiatives, switched to virtual interaction during the

COVID-19 lockdowns. Not only did this break down geographical barriers, offering participation to people living with dementia from across the whole of the United States, but also enabled some form of social interaction at a time of increased and enforced isolation. These classes have continued online, as well as growth of the in-person sessions, emphasising a need for more investment in and expansion of the programme's delivery.

The approach of creating stories instigated from the experiences of those living with dementia expands agency for them and offers a leadership moment. This can break down hierarchies that emerge from being in care relationships and grow confidence for individuals through the agency they develop. Bringing family members and carers into the activity offers a beautiful experience of moving together. Listening and understanding the participants' lived experience and using this to influence how to meet them and support them on their unique journey through classes are core to the approach. This also emphasises the importance of responding to those who are there in the present moment, whichever space or group are meeting.

A big underlying premise behind this work is that dance is an extension of our language and an inherent part of our sense of expression. It is important that the lived experience of those living with dementia is front and centre in the sessions. The practice leads with the belief that people are experts in their own bodies and spaces need to be created where people can meet with the work where they are, in that moment. When you're coming into a community where people's agency has been systematically stripped away, often in medical spaces, the first part of the process is rebuilding this. This begins with framing a sense of safety and scaffolding an experience that people can access in different ways, resisting a one-size-fits-all approach.

> *Because we work in a group setting, there might be some people for whom moving is becoming difficult and others for whom verbal communication is really affected, and one participant may end up creating the words for the group and somebody else leans more into creating the movement. And so we're practising dealing in the group*

> *body. Whether that group body is with just one other body (a duet) or whether that is with a body of ten people, it is understanding that this body of ten people is its own entity. And although it might be made-up of component instruments, the same as our body is made up of component body parts; they each have their own unique way of how they speak, but when we come and work together in this way, we discover a way to speak collectively. (M. Kaczmarska, personal communication, 2024)*

DANCE AS A FORM OF ENTERTAINMENT AND ESCAPISM

In challenging times and environments, people turn to the arts for entertainment and escapism. In the 2008 recession, London theatre's contribution to the UK economy increased (Smith, 2013). Dance is a way to self-reflect and process change, providing an outlet for emotion. It can also help others who are going through the same challenges in life or broaden their mind to another perspective. During the COVID-19 pandemic, TV, online arts programmes and social media platforms such as TikTok supported people's morale. Dance programmes helped people living with health issues to mitigate the effects of social isolation and prevent the worsening of clinical and functional symptoms (Delabary et al., 2022).

There is increasing evidence that dance is a powerful tool for positive wellbeing and health; however, you are engaging with it. Research has shown that those who participated in a creative or cultural activity were 38% more likely to report good health compared to those who did not. For participants who engage with dance, the figure increased to 62% (Leadbetter & O'Connor, 2013). Dance as a creative form of care for ourselves and others can be a means to veer away from the anatomised and medicalised body towards the understanding of the body as a central voice to tell the stories of the shifting and complex nature of being alive.

Maraz et al.'s (2015) development of the Dance Motivation Inventory demonstrates the range of reasons for participation in dance. They highlight that for those specifically taking dance classes as a recreational activity, and not pursued as a profession, 'four additional factors were identified: Mood Enhancement, Self-confidence, Trance and Escapism' (p. 8). This recognises that the individual gains social benefits from dance (self-confidence, trance) as well as the benefits of improving mood and a form of escapism.

Creative, emotional or imaginative escapism can be invaluable for those who find themselves in health environments, offering moments of relief from troubling and sometimes traumatic situations. Dance within medicalised spaces demonstrates how it can not only encourage movement from those needing to develop bodily skills but also offer a transcendental experience. The following case study explores the importance of storytelling and imagination as a way of addressing concerns associated with hospital visits.

A CULTURAL DANCE OFFERING IN MEDICAL ENVIRONMENTS

Akādemi, UK

Akademi have been delivering dance programmes, including *Dance Well*, in London hospitals for over two decades, taking South Asian dance and all that it offers – mindfulness, breathing, relaxation – to hospital wards, hospital staff and hospital visitors. They are one of only a few organisations working with South Asian dance in health settings in the UK.

> *In one particular hospital that we have worked in for over twenty years, we used to do a lunchtime performance at 1pm that would be for anybody and everybody in the atrium downstairs at the hospital. We then shifted to taking a little bit of those performances to the ward for the people who couldn't come down to watch it. So instead of performing an hour-long show, we could take a 5-minute snippet and perform it in the ward in the middle, between the beds. Next that became a workshop, starting with a performance before taking it to the ward with those little moments of movement and performance becoming a bit*

> *more interactive and inclusive. (S. Subramaniam, personal communication, 2024, Artistic Director and Joint-CEO; Akādemi, 2024)*

One of the most beautiful features of South Asian dance that is core to the hospital practice (and the wider work of the company) is storytelling. Subramaniam emphasises how this can be highly gestural, and expressive through the face, making it ideal for working with people in their hospital beds, as seen in Fig. 3. There are positive and inclusive health and wellbeing implications in terms of movement and in only working with gestures. Hand coordination and using some of those gestures to tell stories that are relatable can bring moments of relief or joy during a time of uncertainty. They can be about anything, whether it is packing to go on a holiday, or a story about a Hindu God or it can just be clapping in rhythm and changing the clapping pattern. The performances also use gestures that connect with people as individuals. And with children, the company tends to do a lot of work with play, engaging the imagination in an environment that can be creatively stifling and scary.

Source: Image credit: © Benedict Johnson.

Fig. 3. A Patient Enjoys Being Taught the Delicate and Powerful Hand Gestures from Kathak Dancing During Akademi's Dance Well Workshop for Patients at St. George's Hospital.

Excerpt from 'Breathe Wellbeing Workshop: Indian dance for mind and body' – Rachel Waterman

> *Our dance today takes part in an area called the Punjab in Indian Pakistan and it's an agriculturally, a very rich fertile area. Beautiful green fields and the people there are very loving and very warm. They really enjoy the warmth of life in each other's company. So, that's the setting. Now our dance starts at the beginning of the day, the sunrise. So we're going to put the hands onto the heart, one hand on top of the other. And think of the sun as coming from the chest. We use the hands and lift the chest towards the ceiling, the arms extend to show the reach of the sun and then open to show its shape. The sunlight reflects on the water of the rivers and you use the hands to show the ripples in the water by the side of the riverbank [arms extend sideways to ceiling one at a time], grow beautiful tall trees and when the wind blows, the leaves of the tree flutter gently towards the earth [hands descend with finger gestures one at a time]. (Breathe Arts Health, 2020)*

Akademi's delivery of South Asian dance recognises the importance of a broad cultural offer for those engaging with dance for health. Their work is about taking South Asian dance to anybody and everybody in the space they are working in, giving people access to it and the opportunity to possibly use it as a form of expression themselves. It is a powerful experience for the company to be able to offer this to those who are in hospitals.

Working in hospitals means that the people the company performs for or works with are commonly not the same week to week. And, this is the preferable option, as the company hopes no one is in hospital for longer than needed. This means the dance artists are excellent at adapting workshop content to those who are in front of them in the present moment. This is a key part of their approach. This adaptability also influences music choices. Subramanian recalls a time when a lady asked to have some hip-hop music for the session, so the artist did a big rhythmic section with gestures.

The request was because her son was a DJ and it enabled her to connect to her family while she was separated from them. Giving people access to things that are familiar and that bring them joy is important here.

In evaluating their work, Akademi have found that their hospital sessions have improved balance, developed relationships, encouraged engagement with cultural activities and improved self-confidence, reducing stress and anxiety. But their work is not only for those admitted into the hospital wards but also for the hospital staff and visitors. The staff sessions, particularly during the height of the COVID-19, have been well attended and continue to be so, which emphasises the value of dance engagement for those providing health care as well as those receiving it (read more about other work in this area in Chapter 5).

SUMMARY

We need to highlight that the science of dancing for health is still in its infancy and more research is needed to continue to evidence the claims that this book is making. Nevertheless, researchers agree that dancing interventions can complement conventional treatment. While dancing will not cure someone's cancer, it might help the person to come to terms with its impact on one's body and learn to adapt to it. Dancing together in group sessions with people that share the same predicaments, as we will continue to see in other case studies, helps people find new courage and hope as they find some solace and communal comfort among those who are having similar experiences of a disease or health issue.

This chapter has reviewed literature and current research on dancing for health, covering the areas of physical health, mental wellbeing, social connection and dance as entertainment. We have summarised common features of these discussions and offered case studies that speak to the variety and breadth of dancing for health, within different dance styles, health environments and countries. The cultural perceptions of dance and impact of dancing for the individual, wider society and health services were analysed.

The following chapter will build upon the beneficial aspects of dancing for health that have been introduced in this one. It will include case studies from four different population groups as examples of different practices.

NOTES

1. Thanks to Aline Nogueira Haas for compiling this case study. She writes: 'I would like to thank all the participants from the "Dance for Parkinson's" project because without them, nothing would be possible. I would also like to express my gratitude to my undergraduate and postgraduate students who collaborate with me on this project, especially Marcela dos Santos Delabary, who has been with me since the beginning of the project'. For more information about the Dance for Parkinson's project, please see the Resources chapter.

2. https://dancersgroup.org/2022/06/stories-in-the-moment/.

3

WHO CAN BENEFIT FROM DANCING?

Have you ever seen someone dancing and thought, *I'd love to do that?* Or heard a piece of music that made you want to move your body before second guessing yourself? Or perhaps you've admired a dance scene from a film such as *Flashdance (1983), West Side Story (1961)* or *Devdas (2002)*? These are all entry points for dance, invitations to participate in dance activity. While dance is often showcased in popular media (films, advertisements) and utilised nightly across the world in performance venues, dance is not always an activity of choice for participation, and sometimes, this is due to feeling as though dance is not accessible or 'for me'.

If we ask you to imagine a dancer, what comes to mind? As detailed in previous chapters, we posit that dance can and should be accessible to everyone who has a body, and the benefits of engagement are wide ranging. As dance does not require particular tools or equipment as some other art forms might, it is inclusionary in its very nature. However, we recognise that dance might not be the choice of activity for everyone, with stereotypes of dance and dancers, perceptions of the self and issues of harm in dance's history all contributing to a reluctance to see dance as something for all to participate in. The traditions and history of dance can be viewed as exclusionary and, as some may argue, this exclusion persists today (Cooper Albright, 1997; Dwarika & Haraldsen, 2023; Hassall, 2023; Smith, 2005).

Having explored *why* people should or could dance in previous chapters, this chapter will look at the benefits of dance for four particular populations: adolescents, adults, cultural communities and disabled people. These groups are selected as not only do they span a large majority of the world population, but also there is particular evidence to demonstrate the specific impact of dance on these groups. Exploration of dance for each population group in this chapter is supplemented with a corresponding case study example, which is intended to complement and accompany the case studies presented in the rest of the book.

ADOLESCENTS, ANXIETY AND TIKTOK

Early engagement with dance and movement can enhance the creative and imaginative abilities of children and young people, developing bodily skills, resilience, discipline and social skills. Creative outlets for children of all ages, but particularly teenagers, have been shown to help support their mental health, enabling them to process emotions and combat the negative effects of an overemphasis on technology use. Dance can contribute to the development of gross and fine motor skills, as well as functional movement skills in early childhood (Liya & Katoningsih, 2021). While dance is beneficial for all children and young people, teenagers today face a growing number of emerging and long existing challenges that present developing health concerns.

In this age, children and young people are growing up during a time of unprecedented technological use and impactful social and political uncertainty. Statistics regarding the mental health of young people do not paint a pretty picture. It is estimated that one in seven 10- to 19-year-olds worldwide experience mental health issues, and these often continue on into adulthood (WHO, 2021). The dominance of social media in the lives of young people can be viewed as both exacerbating and relieving the mental health burdens. Social media use for teenagers has become a new way of building and demonstrating social capital and can indicate social influence, shaping behaviour and serving as the new sphere of influence (Dennen et al., 2020). These social media platforms and ways of communicating have also opened new ways of engaging in dance, with TikTok being a source of new dance trends and viral dance routines. While this can be seen as encouraging more dance engagement through recreational platforms (Cervi, 2021), and it is a new means for disseminating dance instruction, the lack of regulation in these spaces means that ensuring the quality and safety of this dance provision is a significant challenge.

Due to its emphasis on creativity, dance is also viewed as a popular physical activity choice for those who might find traditional sports exclusionary or intimidating. Dance is one of the top five choices for physical activity among girls (Youth Sport Trust, 2023) and, by being on the schools National Curriculum in the UK, for example, there is an expectation that young people are introduced to dance at an early age. As the following case study demonstrates, opportunities for young people to dance can significantly impact their mental health and equip them to face the challenges implicit in modern life. Local dance provision is important, emphasising community structures that support teenagers to engage, achieve and sustain healthy and active lifestyles.

TACKLING INEQUALITY AND INACTIVITY FOR YOUNG PEOPLE

Dance Action Zone Leeds (DAZL), UK

According to government statistics, the percentage of 16–17-year-olds not in education, employment or training in Leeds (UK) is 2% higher than the England national average. The number of school pupils claiming free school meals is higher than the national average in both primary and secondary schools. Over a fifth of children and young people in Leeds experience the lowest levels of deprivation according to the Index of Multiple Deprivation. It is also estimated that 31% of children and young people are inactive in Leeds. These statistics are the grounds upon which Dance Action Zone Leeds (DAZL) was created, aiming to tackle inactivity and inequality for children and young people in Leeds.

DAZL offers subsidised dance classes in a range of styles and genres, from lyrical to street dance and contemporary to cheerdance. Community is a hugely significant aspect of their offer, with classes delivered in several areas of Leeds and the surrounding areas, aiding access to dance for young people in these areas. Regional access to dance provision can be difficult, both watching dance as an audience member and taking part in dance classes. DAZL's classes take place both inside and outside of school settings, broadening who can access dance activity in Leeds and breaking down some of the geographic and financial barriers to access.

DAZL directly and openly attends to the growing needs of young people through a programme of dance activity with the aims of addressing physical and mental health. Initially established as a public health initiative in 2000, DAZL aims:

1. To improve the mental and physical health of young people aged 3–19 years, particularly girls, through dance as physical activity in disadvantaged communities of Leeds.
2. To reduce health inequalities, improving the health and wellbeing of children, young adults with disabilities up to 25 years, families and the wider community throughout Yorkshire through asset-based community dance and wider dance opportunities.

The psychological, social and physical impact of DAZL's work on those who participated in the programme has been recognised (Archbold & Bond, 2020). This impact was found to reduce emotional and peer problems, reduce social media use and increase confidence, physical activity levels and friendships on average for the young people who were involved in the DAZL programme. Psychosocial benefits of participation in dance activity that is specifically targeting children and young people, with the purpose of reducing inequalities and improving mental health through a community-based approach, should not be underestimated.

Recognising that, for some young people, exercise offered in school may be their only opportunity for physical activity, DAZL also provides a school holiday dance programme to encourage the continuation of a healthy lifestyle away from the routine of school. This supports the notion that dance should be taught across all ages and stages within education, across the world, not limiting it to only those who have the financial means and geographical access to such activity.

Recognition of the need for opportunities to progress in dance beyond the end of participants' time in the DAZL programme has led to the development of a Community Youth Dance Leaders course that seeks to train and develop new generations of dance teachers, who, DAZL hope, will go on to deliver classes in their local area. As a model of organisational development that has a clear pipeline of engagement and of progression, this course encourages aspiring young dancers to stay active longer and to develop new skills in leadership and teaching. This aspirational approach can be seen to be providing future routes through and beyond the dancing that takes place during adolescence and contributes to understanding that dance can lead to viable career opportunities.

After thinking about the impact and provision of dance for teenagers and young people, the next section will consider what happens when we shift into 'adulthood'.

DANCING THROUGH AND FOR HEALTH EXPERIENCES IN ADULTHOOD

Pablo Picasso once said, 'Everyone is born an artist. The problem is how to remain an artist when we grow up'. A quarter of adults do not meet recommended physical activity levels (WHO, 2022a, 2022b, 2022c, 2022d). While there has been some evidence to suggest a rise in leisure-time physical activity, there is also evidence that work-related physical activity has declined (Hallal et al., 2012). To counteract this decline, dance can act as a fun and creative physical activity, from Zumba and Dancercise classes to traditional ballet or tap classes, or even visiting a Salsa club! Dance offers adults a chance to creatively engage with themselves, their bodies and others. Bodies of research into the benefits of dance for health and wellbeing tend to focus on the developmental stages of childhood and the physiological and social experiences of older adults, as detailed earlier in this chapter. Less attention is paid to the experience of adults; no longer children but not yet viewed as 'elderly'.

Carving out time to engage with the self through dance is a valuable and impactful choice. However, research into dance for the general adult population is limited, and there is evidence that demonstrates a significant drop in physical activity for individuals once they leave school and enter the workforce. Particular working patterns and the pressures of adult life can leave us with little time for recreational endeavours or physical activity, which is one of the key global health challenges (Fong Yan et al., 2018). Positive effects of recreational dance include stress relief, greater relaxation and improved overall wellbeing, which can lead to greater productivity and work performance (Vecchi et al., 2022). More significantly, there is a correlation between physical activity in childhood and physical activity as an adult, impacting on health outcomes and the public health of the population. Infrequent participation in sports at school age is associated with physical inactivity in adulthood (Tammelin et al., 2003; Telama et al., 2005), suggesting that the work of organisations like DAZL (above) is important for tackling inactivity not only in adolescence but also in adulthood.

In addition to a decline in physical activity, there is some evidence that shows a significant decline in creativity in later adulthood (Hui et al., 2019). Adults with creative thinking, processing and behaviour skills 'contribute to society by translating their original ideas into projects with social impact' (Hui et al., 2019, p. 70). Dancing can provide a creative outlet for adults to explore artistic expression and develop divergent thinking. It should be noted that the evidence concerning creative decline in adulthood is broad strokes, and there is some research that suggests more is needed to consider the different domains and types of creativity in order to better understand the nuance and application of this creative decline over the lifespan (Weinstein et al., 2014). Our creative capacity can change over time and develop depending on the strategies used to engage creativity, one of which can be dancing (Romaniuk & Romaniuk, 1981).

Dancing as an adult can also address many developing social and mental health-related issues. The next case study will explore the experience of dancing for a population group who have lived experience of cancer, a specific medical condition that mostly affects adults, an example of the growing corpus of dance classes designed for community groups with a shared lived experience or communal interests.

MOVING, DANCING AND FEELING THROUGH EXPERIENCES OF CANCER

Move Dance Feel

In 2013, it was reported that 25% of people experiencing poor health or disability in the UK had been treated for cancer in their past (Macmillan Cancer Support, 2013). The long-term consequences of cancer can affect physical and mental health, as well as relationships. Common effects include chronic fatigue, sexual challenges, bodily swelling, pain, peripheral neuropathy, anxiety and worry, insomnia, body image disturbances, weight changes, loneliness and gastrointestinal issues, which can greatly impact people's quality of life. This is information that encouraged Emily Jenkins to start Move Dance Feel in 2016, offering dance to women living with or beyond cancer, as well as to women caring for someone with cancer (Fig. 4).

> *My intention is to unite people in a safe space where the focus is on creativity and our relationship with our bodies, which is inherent to dance. Move Dance Feel is a place of exploration, curiosity and joy where we can move in a way that feels positive and playful. I know from past experiences personally and also in the work that I do that there's strength in simply bringing people together. (E. Jenkins, personal communication, Move Dance Feel Founder, 2024)*

The negative side effects post cancer treatment can be significantly debilitating, but can go largely unsupported by the medical system, who deem people 'cured' when in remission. In reality, those who have had cancer treatment can be living with constant pain or anxiety, with very high rates of depression, people on anti-depressants, loneliness, body image dysmorphia, insomnia and

Source: Photo by Camilla Greenwell.

Fig. 4. Move Dance Feel CIC, Dance in Cancer Care. Founder Emily Jenkins.

the list goes on. These experiences are often hidden, and access to treatment can be patchy. Move Dance Feel offers a physical invitation to move with others who have shared experiences or collective understandings of cancer, while acknowledging how each cancer journey is unique.

During cancer treatment, language about the body is troubling and this is often reflected in societal discourse around cancer. Jenkins recognises that it can be seen as radical to dance with people experiencing intense health situations where the body is often spoken about as problematic, broken or attacking. Her intention is to offer accessible dance experiences, in which people can work against the preconceptions that dance is associated with perfectionist tendencies or aesthetic values. The emphasis is on how dance and movement feels, which is nodded to in the company's name.

> *The cognitive overwhelm associated with cancer diagnosis, and all the emotions that come with it, means there's so much going on cerebrally that it's difficult for people to reach a calm place of mind needed for healing or wellness.*

> *Sometimes you have to release physically, and physically move through the overwhelming feelings, to actually enable things to shift. This caught my attention. When cancer is so intense for the body, causing radical changes, why do people not start with the body as a way to reconnect, soothe, re-sensitise and calm the nervous system? In parallel to that, I found loads of evidence around the benefits of physical activity in this context – proving to be advantageous and recommended at all stages. So whether you've just been diagnosed, and dance as part of prehabilitation, or if undergoing treatment and being physically active you can respond better to treatment, maintain better levels of well-being and post treatment can in some cases prevent recurrence. (E. Jenkins, personal communication, 2024)*

Move Dance Feel participants have emphasised that dancing has had positive shifts in how they connect to and perceive their bodies. This seems to reject a medical model of 'curing', 'restoring' or 'improving' the body, but rather offers an opportunity to appreciate the body as it is, and what it *can do*. Experiences of stress and anxiety seem to be significantly alleviated by participation in Move Dance Feel sessions, and key reported outcomes are feelings of accomplishment, confidence and connection.

> *I have learnt to appreciate my body – to break away from not trusting it and being afraid of being in it. (Move Dance Feel participant)*

> *I have been able to explore how we can both express feelings that perhaps have no other outlet but really importantly, challenge me to explore moving in new ways that are not patterned. This seems to be opening a wider sense of creativity [and] new brain pathways in other areas of life. (Move Dance Feel participant)*

The dancing is complemented by social time as well, which consolidates relationships between those participating. Where dance catalyses trust and intimacy, talking time reinforces this and emphasises its importance when moving through a sense of vulnerability together.

DANCE PRACTICE TO IMPROVE UNDERSTANDING OF HEALTH IN SPECIFIC CULTURAL CONTEXTS

Cultural difference between healthcare services and their users is one of the barriers of successful health intervention within the increasingly more diverse societies of our contemporary global world (Darivemula et al., 2021). Dance is an effective medium to develop the cultural competency of health professionals. It has also been evidenced that people stick better at a physical activity when it is tied to their specific cultural heritage (Vahabi & Damba, 2015; Whitehorse et al., 1999). Culturally oriented dance is practised within a community or group which can be formed out of diverse origins. In addition to influencing positive physical, mental, and social health among participants, cultural dances such as African or Asian dance serve several purposes related to traditional practices, cultural transmission, social acceptance and connectedness (O'Conner, 2021).

Learning a dance which engages with the group members' personal histories and culture facilitates diverse participation and collaborations. It improves community cohesion and health literacy through building relationships and understanding of bodily processes. It is an activity whereby health professionals and community members can exchange and mutually learn to contextualise their understanding of health. For example, in many non-western cultures (such as African and Asian culture), the significance of spirituality and the connection to one's spirit is viewed as essential for healing to take place. Body and mind must be united through dance to facilitate healing. As such dance is embedded in a practice of self-esteem and offers an alternative cathartic experience for not only individuals but also the community as a whole (O'Conner, 2021).

In contrast, carers, dance and health professionals need to be able to respect cultural differences to improve participation and inclusion to health interventions. Although most cultural and belief systems embraced dance in their practice, some religions have controlled or banned dancing for various reasons. Its relation with the body and sexuality can be seen as threatening and be censored in some cultures (Hanna, 2017). For different religious and cultural reasons, people might feel unable or reluctant to participate in some of the activities. For example, participants may not feel allowed to take part in dance as a performance or in its representation of any living form through the dance narrative (see also the Akādemi case study in Chapter 2). Cultural dance for health sessions needs to be flexible and adaptable for all the participants.

The next case study will focus on two specific aspects of cultural dance: the use of music and rhythms and group formations.

WORKING WITH DIVERSE COMMUNITY GROUPS

Moving Tu Dance, UK

Sandra Golding delivers African holistic dance as a complimentary therapeutic community dance movement education in the Midlands. Since the 1980s, Golding's dance practice, which is rooted in African Caribbean traditions, has been helping a wide range of communities to improve their health, including children with disabilities, older people and people from African heritage. As a first-generation African Caribbean woman, Golding argues that dance and health interventions are not often led by people of African and Caribbean heritage, for people of African and Caribbean heritage.

While dance artists generally have a good intention towards the people they want to work with, they can be over-eager to share their practice at the expense of establishing relationships. For Golding, building trust is a first step towards healthier communities. Taking the time to create relationships is essential. Identifying who the key players in the community are, who they need to know – community workers, group leaders – will be important to initiate conversations with local groups.

Similarly, the longevity of a project can be a challenge to deliver a successful health and wellbeing community dance project. While piloting an activity for a shorter time can allow a relevant period of evaluation in order to calibrate an activity (usually between 6 and 12 weeks), questioning the continuity and sustainability of a project is important. What happens when the project finishes? What happens to the community? (S. Golding, personal communication, 2024).

Golding uses her lived experience as a community worker, a creative artist and somatic practitioner to create long-term relationships inside and outside of the dance studio. Setting collective and individual intentions at the outset of each class, she calibrates the emotional needs of the group. Similarly, by introducing basic African Caribbean movement, she can assess the degree of rhythmical competency of each participant and get anyone to dance regardless of their physical ability or cultural background. She also develops performance opportunities to showcase her work in the community including co-creation pieces performed in collaboration with her intergenerational community class groups (30–60 years old). Mutual support is at the heart of these enjoyable experiences which forge long-term friendship groups.

The role of music is central in her work to help people reconnect with their cultural heritage and/or their bodies. There is little opportunity to dance with live music in mainstream dance classes. Some of her classes' participants might never have danced with live music before. Music and dance connect people together, but the combination of both forms offers an embodied way to learn more about the cultural heritage of the movement. Golding provides historical contexts of the development of the dance to challenge Eurocentric perceptions of African Caribbean dance.

For instance, the use of the circle in group dancing is introduced as a central space in African Caribbean culture and as a way of coming together, celebrating and inviting self-expression. Golding offers connection with its modern day use in Hip-Hop dance. Similarly, she introduces specific African Caribbean drum patterns or body drumming at the beginning of a class to facilitate communication, cooperation and creativity in the group. Research has evidenced that the rush of beneficial hormones produced by group drumming can reduce depression and anxiety and improve social resilience (Fancourt et al., 2016). Participants feel invigorated and ready for more dancing.

The class continues with further cultural references to group formations. In her dance and wellbeing group for women over 60 years old, she uses quadrille and line dancing to introduce the complex historical contexts of the forms and their relationships with European court dancing and slavery. People work in pairs, change places and work with counts following more rhythmical patterns, with the use of diverse genres of music (from pop to reggae to music played by more traditional instruments such as the kora). These group dance ensembles help with balance and coordination but also stimulate brain memory. They bring a joyful sense of togetherness (S. Golding, personal communication, 2024).

Golding offers further development in her class by progressively integrating her somatic approach. Participants are introduced to anatomical and physiological aspects of the dance. In order to connect to the body more deeply, Golding uses visualisation and images of nature to explore different qualities of movements which engage participants in memory processes. With eyes closed, focusing on breathing, visually tracking organs, while associating natural elements such as images of a tree or sky, participants become more relaxed to embody their movements, as demonstrated in Fig. 5. This deep listening of the body enables participants to identify any source of discomfort and find more ease in the body to work around it.

According to Golding, this process leads participants to experience a therapeutic sense of self-expression. They feel more

Source: Photo credit: Courtesy of artist.

Fig. 5. Sandra Golding Teaching.

confidence to approach their doctors to communicate more clearly about pain and discomfort in their body. One participant reflects on how his relationship with dance has changed since working with Golding,

> *From initial indifference to a realisation that dancing can express your deepest thoughts and emotions. A gesture or movement can convey feelings that would be hard to put into words! It feels good to be expressing these things which hadn't necessarily surfaced but were contributing to a general feeling of anxiety before the session. Very therapeutic! (Workshop participants in Golding, 2023)*

While somatics may not be a well-known term in the African Caribbean community, Golding argues that the process of deep listening involved in African Caribbean dance is somatic. Depending on their background, participants are able to reconnect to their cultural movement or experience the dance as a way to break down cultural barriers. This can lead to a deep sense of healing.

THE ASSUMPTION OF THERAPY: DANCE AND DISABLED PEOPLE

Philosophy of dance is increasingly grappling with its history and traditions that have focused 'on bodily perfection, which privileges abled bodies as those that can best make and perform dance as art' (Hall, 2018, p. 1). Cultural studies scholar Owen Smith (2005) describes the traditionally idealised dancing body as an 'erect, physically defined "Apollonian" form (privileged as the noble and honourable body in discourses that produced dance as a theatrical form)' (p. 77). This historic impression of a statuesque, standing, God-like body being the 'ideal' body for dance, that can be seen as dominating the shared cultural psyche, is exclusionary. But, there has long been an eagerness to shift away from this image of a 'normative' dancer and use the 'subversive potential' of the body to increase participation and engagement in dance (Adair, 1992, p. 24).

Often, when people think about movement activity for disabled people, it is assumed that it must be for therapeutic purposes, to alleviate or manage symptoms associated with impairments (Benjamin, 2010). There is a growing practice of inclusive dance provision around the world, however, that advocates for dance as a creative, recreational and expressive activity for disabled people that just happens to have secondary therapeutic benefits. This is not to say that there is no place and purpose for dance-based therapeutic interventions (see the discussion regarding DMT and DMP in Chapter 1), but it should not always be assumed that dancing for disabled people is therapy, as this is not the immediate assumption for any other dancing population group.

Research indicates and evidences the benefits of dance for disabled people (Cherriere et al., 2020; May et al., 2021; Prieto et al., 2020), but it has been highlighted that it is generally of poor quality with gaps in provision, and it is proposed that more research is necessary with measurable outcomes and robust methodologies (May et al., 2021; Pontone et al., 2021). This can be in tension with the principles and values of community dance activity that tends to favour subjective, collective and lived experience of dance.

Physical activity for disabled people can often be conducted or imposed within medical environments or through a medical model of disability that can be traumatic. Experience of physical discomfort, like that experienced after intense dance activity, can be associated with previous experiences of 'interventions to "normalise" [a person's] body usage by physiotherapists and other medical practitioners' (Whatley, 2007, p. 10). Inclusive dance, emerging from the community dance movements of the 1980s, can offer a different environment for movement activity and an approach that centres the individual's experience and needs in a more democratic atmosphere, working to undo or recalibrate people's relationship to/with physical activity.

The final case study in this chapter spotlights an inclusive disabled-led dance organisation that seeks to improve the health and wellbeing of all their participants, widening access to and understanding of dance for disabled people.

ADDRESSING HEALTH INEQUALITIES FOR PEOPLE WITH LEARNING DISABILITIES

DanceSyndrome, UK

DanceSyndrome is an inclusive and disability-led dance company based in the north-west of England. Founded in 2013 out of frustration at the lack of opportunities for work in dance for disabled people, mother and daughter duo Sue and Jen Blackwell have worked to build an influential company that offers, among many other things, weekly or one-off dance sessions for all who want to 'improve their health, wellbeing and confidence – regardless of age or ability' (DanceSyndrome, 2024).

Core to DanceSyndrome's mission is co-production and co-delivery, seeking to create pathways of opportunity for all people who want to participate in dance activity (Fig. 6). This includes improving life chances and health outcomes for people with learning disabilities. While this sometimes addresses the physical aspects of health through engagement in dance as a physical activity, it also recognises the importance of developing confidence and communication skills alongside social engagement as being core to living healthy and fulfilled lives.

DanceSyndrome highlights dance as a recreational, life-affirming activity as well as something that can offer a pathway to work for those who seek it. By focusing on dance as opportunity-building, DanceSyndrome resists the view of dance as simply a therapeutic health endeavour for people with disabilities, a view which many practitioners included in this book have and as we will continue to demonstrate. Instead, improving health outcomes and life chances are rather byproducts of engagement with person-centred dance activity that focuses primarily on co-production, individual needs and a caring approach.

Sharing the practice and experience of DanceSyndrome staff and co-producers with healthcare professionals is also a key aspect of their developing practice,

> *DanceSyndrome [are committed to] changing perceptions of disabled people. Working with aspiring Dance Artists*

Source: Photo credit: William Fisher.

Fig. 6. DanceSyndrome Workshop.

> *and future health and social care professionals before they start their careers encourages them to think about inclusivity without the bias that may already be established in some organisations and gives hope for a more inclusive future. (Blackwell & Blackwell, 2023, p. 39)*

This sharing of practice has extended to the production of a series of videos created in partnership with NHS England. The videos seek to communicate six features of DanceSyndrome's approach: Everybody Dance, Dance by Example, the Importance of the Individual, Adaptation, Connection and Creativity. The project seeks to encourage the inclusion of these features into the daily practice of nursing and care staff and 'demonstrate the many ways that people with learning disabilities can live fulfilled lives, contributing to society and becoming visible leaders, performers, and advocates' (DanceSyndrome, 2022).

Advocating for yourself and your own health needs is a complex task, and, for those who have challenges with communication and confidence, advocating and communicating your health needs can be extremely challenging. DanceSyndrome, as an inclusive dance organisation, helps develop agency in those who participate, empowering them not only to be more attune with their own bodies and bodily management but also to advocate for their needs and wants.

SUMMARY

While this chapter has looked at the specific benefits of dance for four population groups, we advocate dancing for all. The ideas presented in the rest of the chapters detail the impact of dance for older people, people with specific health conditions and those who are reluctant to engage in dance for multiple and varied reasons. What is key is that all people have access to dance and the opportunity to explore whether it is the creative, active, social activity for them. The case study examples have raised important considerations such as the importance of community and offering alternative approaches that avoid medicalised language and raise aspirations. The following chapter will explore *how* an individual can participate in dancing for health, at home, outdoors, with a partner or in a group.

4

HOW CAN I ENGAGE WITH DANCE?

This chapter focuses on how individuals can engage with dancing by outlining a range of practical tools. It offers further insights into the benefits of dance in specific contexts including at home, online and even outdoors. It begins by offering methods of dance for the purposes of relaxation, as well as some strategies to bring daily reflections into your life. To this end, we suggest keeping a diary to record positive changes in your mood, energy and endurance. There are some activities addressing dancing with music, objects, children, young people, adults and older people. They can be undertaken either alone or with the support of family/carers. We have separated solo, partner and group practices into different sections. At the end of the chapter, we offer further ideas and examples of how to experience dance as performers or observers.

Each practice introduced in this chapter is underpinned by research that evidences the range of processes at work when dancing, such as synchronicity and sensorial and social bonding. The practical elements can be read in conjunction with the resources section, which references the sources of some of the activities, suggests further reading and provides useful links including a themed music playlist.

Inclusive dance is good practice (Marsh & Whatley, 2017). The tasks below support approaches to inclusive dance. In some cases, we have adopted Stopgap Dance Company's inclusive methodology to offer a possible 'translation' of tasks for people who may require adaptations. 'Translation is the skill of finding a correlative version of a movement by someone who has a different physicality to you' (Stopgap Dance, 2024).

HEALTHY PRACTICE

There are some health and safety considerations when engaging in dance in your home:

- Always allow time for a warm-up and cool down. We offer one example of each that can be used by anyone, but there are lots of other examples out there.
- Check that you have enough space around you to move safely. Check suitability of furniture or other equipment at home. For example, if you are using a chair, is it sturdy?
- Wear appropriate clothing and footwear for moving.
- You know your body best. Make sure you pay attention to what it is telling you as you participate in these activities. If you are unsure about anything, seek support from a family member, carer or a medical or dance professional.

AT HOME

In this section, we suggest some ideas to be active and creative through dancing in the comfort of your own home. We have evidenced that dance can make a positive contribution to the lives of people needing long-term care. According to the World Health Organisation, in Europe, around 80% of long-term care is provided informally by family members, neighbours, friends or community members who are often unpaid. In countries where long-term care systems are not as well-developed or resourced, the amount of care provided informally is likely to be even higher (WHO, 2022d, December 1).

Furthermore, in order to tackle the current international health crisis whereby half of the world lacks essential health services, the WHO recommends self-care interventions.

> *Self-care interventions are tools which support the ability of individuals, families and communities to promote health, prevent disease, maintain health, and cope with illness and disability with or without the support of a health worker. (WHO, 2022a, 2022b, 2022c, 2022d)*

Dance as an evidence-based self-care intervention can contribute to the support of individuals as active agents in managing their own health care outside and inside their home with or without a carer. Dance home practice allows people to access the benefits of dance when they otherwise might not be able to do so. There are several reasons that this might be the case: you might not be able to travel outside of your home or you may live in an isolated environment; or it might be that you are not comfortable taking classes in public or that you don't have much time for yourself due to working or caring responsibilities. You might live in a country where access to dance is not widely available or dance might be less culturally accepted. Dancing at home could be a good solution under any of these circumstances. In this chapter, we offer specific recommendations and some examples for engaging with dance at home including through online dancing.

Dance for Relaxation, Inspiration and Reflection

- Chair or standing relaxation inspired by 'the small dance'. (This can be used for a warm-up.)

This exercise is an adaptation of a well-known practice in contemporary dance from the influential American choreographer Steve Paxton. He was the founder of Contact Improvisation, a dance form practised around the world (the starting point of the practice can be described as two bodies sharing weight through a moving point of physical contact). This practice invites us to pay attention to our world of small movement – what Paxton has called 'the small dance', the incessant shifts that are happening in our bodies all the time, below everyday awareness. American dancer and educator Emilie Conrad defined movement as a core expression of life. For her, 'we are movement'. The small dance is the practice of noticing how our bodies feel, move and respond to what is going on around us. Originally, the dance was performed standing up (Paxton, 2008), but we have adapted it to be performed seated. You can find the audio score in the resource links.

I recommend voice recording the text, delivering it slowly with pauses between each sentence and then playing it when you want to practise. You could also ask someone to read it for you.

Sitting on a chair

Place your hand on each side of the chair.

Inhale, thinking of your favourite fragrance.

Continue inhaling that scent for three more breaths.

Feel your shoulders releasing their weight downwards.

Focus internally on your face.

Relax your eyes (you may choose to close them if comfortable).

Imagine a line between your ears.

That is where your spine begins.

Make a very small 'yes' motion with the head.

Make a very small 'no' motion with the head.

Move your attention to your lungs.

Breathe from the bottom of your lungs.

Expand your ribcage out, up and back.

Each breath offers a gentle massage to your intestines.

As you relax your whole body,

Feel the weight of your head.

Feel the sense of gravity on the chair.

As your muscles relax you will feel the sensation of gravity.

Feel the way that your arms are hanging.

Following the arms' downward direction.

Initiate a very small stretch.

Aiming for less rather than more,

Keep following the sensation of the gravity as you shift the weight of your stretches.

Keep tuning into your small dance.

You keep relaxing and it's holding you up.

Shift the weight from side to side, engage the feet, legs.

If possible, you may get up from the chair,

Progressively shifting the sense of gravity onto the legs.

Keep small stretches connected to the gravity and the weight of your body parts.

After few minutes, slow down movement.

Come progressively into stillness when it feels right.

- Creating portraits

Standing or sitting still.

Close your eyes and let your hands scan your body's contours. Touch every part of the body with special attention to the parts that you cannot see.

Write down your experience and save them as a series of portraits as you repeat the practice regularly.

- Dancing the highlight of your day

Sit or lie down comfortably.

Close your eyes if it is comfortable.

Think about your day.

From all the images that your memory generates, choose one.

Focus on it for a while. Seek out movements that represent the image or event that you have chosen. Perform these movements.

Dancing with Music

Music has the power to bring us through time and space. It can trigger a flood of memories and associated emotions. People suffering from a loss of memory who might not be able to recognise their loved ones may remember the melody of a song. This is because the part of the brain that processes musical information remains intact even when other parts of memory have degenerated (Elliot & Gardner, 2018). Furthermore, listening to music can stimulate different areas of the brain. Indeed, research has proven that listening to music is one of the most powerful ways to change the structure of one brain. Music can have a positive impact on our hormonal balance, concentration and mood, and it can boost our immune system (Rebecchini, 2021).

Listening to music often makes us move. In their book *Dancing is the Best Medicine*, Christensen and Chang (2021) define rhythms as a key factor in the health benefits of dance. They reveal that in the brain, listening and moving are linked: 'Dance and rhythms are inseparable, with rhythm forming the link between music and dance' (Christensen & Chang, 2021, p. 27). They further evidence that together music and movement increase the production of endorphins that makes us relax, happy. Moving feels easy. These moments bring us joy and physical wellbeing (Christensen & Chang, 2021, p. 111).

- Dancing to your favourite music (solo/partner/group)

Put on your selected piece of music.

Dance to it by including different body parts one by one: head, hands, arms, torso, legs and feet – use movements trying to engage with as many body parts as possible (standing or sitting).

Try without the music and follow the rhythm of your breath. (This can be used as a warm-up.)

- Development for working with music.

This task is inspired by Hanna Picket's improvisation exercises (see resources)

Select two music tracks – choose at least one genre of music that you are not familiar with.

Listen to the music and let it affect the way you move.

Think about using a mixture of body parts, a change of levels (standing, seating, lying) and a change of direction (changing the side of the room you are facing).

Then repeat the task with the second track.

Explore with changing speed of movement and focusing on only one body part.

***Self-reflection or discussion with a group**: How does the music affect the way you move? How do you move to the tempo and rhythm of the music? Does the way you move change with the second track?*

Online Dancing

One of the positive things that the COVID-19 pandemic helped to encourage was a rise in online access to dance activity. The online possibilities increased exponentially. There is now a plethora of interactive digital initiatives that people can engage with to participate in dance at home. Online dancing erases borders and breaks down a number of barriers (although we do acknowledge the digital barrier to access here). It is now possible to participate in classes with an Argentine tango teacher from the intimacy of your home or to get your children dancing with online programmes run or designed by dance professionals around the world. Some of these classes are specifically designed as inclusive practice for disabled and non-disabled children and adults. Take an online dance inspired class – there are many styles to choose from and relevant resources are signposted and referenced in the 'useful links' section. Below is one example of an online inclusive dance practice programme for individual home practice:

- Adaptive methods of movement for disabled and non-disabled adults.

Stopgap Dance: Inclusion Elevates Everyone

Drawing on Stopgap's 25 years of experience, Stopgap's online classes share some key elements of inclusive dance and choreography for people to dance at home. Stopgap's Home Practice series is a self-guided programme of inclusive contemporary dance classes and workshops that introduce a variety of approaches to inclusive dance practice, working with your own body, learning style, disability and experience. Stopgap advises that Home Practice is not about imitating what happens in the dance studio but instead focuses on a solo experience in a class context in order to build confidence without the pressure of being watched.

Some of the classes are designed to boost motivation and movement in the morning or as a mid-afternoon slump buster, while other classes offer more specific technical insights into the Stopgap Dance choreographic process. See the links to the online classes in the resources section.

OUTDOOR DANCING

The beneficial effect of nature and its positive contribution to people's mood has been clearly evidenced by research (Beute & de Kort, 2014). It is now also evidenced that dancing outside increases positive emotion when compared to the same practice indoors (Byrka & Ryczko, 2018).

The following task assumes that you are in an outdoor environment and uses it to inspire movements (as represented in Fig. 7).

Examine the details of the space you find yourself in.

Observe above your head, below your feet.

What is in the space? What can you see?

Start following the lines and curves of the space to initiate movement.

Source: Photo credit: Courtesy of the artist.

Fig. 7. Mottisfont Residency 2014, Devised for Screendance Art Film 'The Greeting', Directed by Lizzie Sykes, Featuring 11 Older Performers Including Meg Edgar and Roland Challis.

Can you dance with a tree? Move with the clouds in the sky?

Look at the shapes of the landscape. Create a duet with it.

Use your body to respond to the lines of a building.

Allow moments to stop, pause and examine the space again.

Think about using a range of body parts to explore the space.

Use headphones to listen to inspiring music while you move with the natural elements.

DANCING WITH CHILDREN AND YOUNG PEOPLE

As we have demonstrated earlier in this book, encouraging a child's natural need to move will boost their motivation and increase their coordination and interpersonal skills. Children dancing use more multimodal skills than when practising other types of sport, as dancing simultaneously draws upon listening, watching, moving, anticipation and adjustment skills (Christensen & Chang, 2021, p. 193). These processes require flexibility, coordination, strength and stamina. Games based on rhythms and simple routines allow children to develop a personal awareness of their bodies which, in turn, can improve their sense of safety. While there can be elements of competition in dancing, we recommend keeping it playful, valuing creativity through movement for its own sake.

Moving to music is conducive to children's self-expression and it can be a simple framework to encourage free improvised movement activity such as spinning, skipping, stamping or flying like a bird, plane or leaf. Open structured improvisation can allow children to use their imagination to become whatever they want at that moment in time. They are allowed to follow non-linear movement, direction and outcomes – in contrast to the predictabilities of linear processes which children are often subjected to. When young people have the freedom to move as they wish, they develop the skill of non-verbal expression which can support them in coping with the emotional upheavals of their daily lives, as detailed in Chapter 3.

The Feather Dance

For this exercise, use long coloured craft feathers and calm music. It exercise works well with a group of intergenerational participants. In Fig. 8, you can see the joy of a grandmother and her grandchild dancing together.

Give one feather to each child and each other participant.

Encourage the children to blow on the feather and follow its movement.

Each child can develop a duet with their feather.

Then they can start exchanging their feather with someone else through breath and movement.

Playfully children and carers try to not let the feathers drop down to the floor.

Source: Photo credit: Noyale Colin.

Fig. 8. Intergenerational Dance Project Led by Diane Amans at the University of Winchester, November 2019.

PARTNER DANCING

Partner dancing is a key element of social occasions in many cultures around the world, such as weddings, birthdays, carnivals and school proms. Television has also recently contributed to a renewed interest in partner dance. Almost eight million people watched the 2019 US final of *Dancing with the Stars*. The UK version, *Strictly Come Dancing*, challenges the way that people think about gender pairing and disability in dance (Stamp, 2022). The positive message of these TV shows is that everybody can learn to dance.

Sharing dance with someone is also about trust and confidence, especially if body lifts are involved as in acrobatic rock'n'roll or Lindy Hop dances. There is a degree of risk and danger that you need to be ready to take together. It involves playing with closeness and distance while being in the present moment so that you can anticipate each other's next move. Partner dancing is like having a meaningful conversation. Regular practice can help develop these transferable interpersonal coordination skills.

One of the most fascinating things about partner dancing is the way that bodies seem to know how to synchronise to each other without having to use words. This happens because our brain can mirror and anticipate movements. One current evolutionary theory of dance posits that dance evolved as a form of interpersonal coordination, which includes both imitation (matching of movements) and synchrony (matching of time). Synchronisation of movement between individuals has been shown to enhance mood, memory performance, coordination, cooperation, affiliation and altruistic behaviour (Basso, 2021, p. 9). Most partner dances have a leader and a follower. Yet eventually, it all becomes a unified, fluid movement – thanks to our brain mirroring capacity.

- Initiating contact and dancing with objects

Human beings need to be touched to be healthy. Research shows that touch is essential to our human sense of belonging. It is the first sense that we develop as a foetus (Brendtro, 2017). Touch triggers biomechanical responses in the body (dopamine and oxytocin hormones) which make us feel good. Having physical contact with each other through dancing is a wonderful opportunity to feel a healing sense of connectivity (Christensen & Chang, 2021). However, touch is loaded with complex private and cultural emotions, and negotiating these feelings can be challenging. It brings us back to intimate relations and positive or negative experiences that we might have had in our life. It is important to take time to develop a sense of safety and respect around contact in dance. While touch might be beneficial and can create an immediate connection without the need for words or explanations when working with others, we need to make sure that touch is accepted and comes as an offer rather than as an imposition.

Before moving onto exercises that involve working with others, you might want to consider this way of exploring contact, which uses balloons or a light ball, to practise working with touch:

Focus on the balloon and start to move.

Create a duet with the balloon.

Play with balancing the balloon on different parts of your body.

Continue by using the balloon to lightly tap your own body.

Think about different types of touch (patting, rubbing, pushing, squeezing, brushing, rolling).

Aim to keep your focus on the balloon.

Explore, with different body parts in contact with the balloon, a range of body parts (hands, arms, legs).

Create a duet with another object (e.g. a scarf or feather).

Improvisation Duets

The mirror improvisation exercise is foundational to partner dance and develops bonding and empathy through movement synchronicity. The instruction is very simple, and this can be done in silence or with music, with people of all ages, with or without an audience. I have provided a preparatory exercise to the mirror improvisation in order to stimulate and practise one of the key communication senses – visual gazing. However, I have also offered an alternative way of practising synchronicity with a partner if using visual gazing is not possible.

Mirror dancing invites partners to simultaneously perceive, accept and respond no matter whether they are leader or followers (Zaporah, 1995, p. 48). It creates a bond between the partners by connecting their bodies and minds. The attention required in this practice allows for a merging of consciousness through a co-activation of the brains. By concentrating on watching the followers (or sensing through touch), the leader is able to pick up on clues to follow. Similarly, the follower's sustained attention in mirroring can lead to the development of the movements. According to neuroscientists, both brains simulate each partner's movement at the same time as if it was one system. This process is not only happening in dancing but also occurring frequently in other everyday circumstances in which group cohesion and team spirit are required. Partner dancing develops the 'mimicry process' of the brain, which increases our ability to understand other people's emotions and intentions, and to be ultimately better able to empathise with them (Christensen & Chang, 2021).

- Focus in/eyes out

Standing or sitting face to face with a partner.

Watch your partner's breath and pay attention to your own.

While you are looking directly at your partner, bring your attention/focus back inside your own body as if you were looking out from the back of your own skull.

(a blurring of vision might occur)

Now gradually shift your attention out until you are looking directly at your partner's face and into their eyes.

Project your energy out through your eyes and into the eyes of your partner.

Do this more and more until you feel like a laser beam is blasting energy out from your eyes into your partner's eyes and into their head.

Now bring your focus slightly back towards yourself.

Move your focus back and forth between the back of your head, your partner's eyes and yours, like a pendulum.

Gradually let your focus settle in the middle, right between your partner's eyes and the back of your skull.

Stay there and become familiar with that sensation.

Exchange with your partner to share the experience of inner and outer attention, reflecting on what felt more like your habitual tendency.

- Mirror dancing (two people)

Standing or sitting face to face, look directly into each other's eyes.

Balance your attention evenly between you and your partner (recalling previous exercises' in and out focus). Choose one person to lead and one person to follow.

The leader will start by initiating any movement and the follower begins mirroring the leader by synchronising to the leader's movements.

Switch roles a couple of times.

Instruction to Develop Mirroring Practice

Leader, explore using slow movement so that the follower can synchronise the timing of the movement in such a way that an outsider would not be able to see who is leading or following.

Leader, explore using movement and facial expressions, projects internal feelings, attitudes, and their state of mind. This can be very playful but should remain focused. Visualise your partner as different people or things that can provoke you. Respond to what you have projected on your partner.

Follower, let the leader's body do the above without thinking about it. You are the mirror image of the person in front of you. Notice the details of your partner's body, including their face.

Leader and follower, experience what your partner is experiencing (feelings) and mirroring back. If the leader looks away, then the follower must look away too.

Then Explore with No Leader and No Follower

Stop what you are doing and start moving in a completely different way.

Slow down.

Don't worry about eye contact anymore.

Once the duet is established, move at any speed and travel through the room.

Translation

If mirroring through gazing is not possible, then try mirroring through touch.

Starting with hands, follow each other's movement.

As the leader, you can also describe verbally what you are doing if speaking is possible.

The same principle of synchronising movement applies, and continuing with the description might not be necessary as the duet becomes one unit moving.

GROUP DANCING: COMMUNITY AND BELONGING

To be happy we need the community of others. Feeling that we belong is essential for our health and wellbeing. Group dancing has the advantage that dancers are not dependent on one partner. Being part of a larger group allows for limitless possibilities. Learning with others allows us to shift roles and responsibilities, as well as having the support of others to develop ideas. The dynamic of the group supports a collective energy. The experience of joy and pleasure in dancing together bonds people and offers a unique feeling of belonging.

Similar to partner dancing, synchronicity is beneficial when dancing in a group. When moving in unison (the same movement at the same time), we feel like a united organism. Studies have evidenced a relationship between the dancers who feel the most synchronicity with the group and the people who felt the most sense of belonging (von Zimmermann, 2018). This feeling is reinforced when people dance together to music. It is further demonstrated that the exertion felt when dancing in synchrony can raise participants' pain threshold and further encourage social bonding (Tarr et al., 2015).

Community Classes and Dance Project

Trained dance practitioners from across the country are commonly found working in community settings and provide accessible and local dance classes for communities. These classes range from early years classes to older people's groups. Dance classes are not only offered in dance schools. Dance teachers will also deliver classes in a wide range of settings including sports associations, clubs or church halls. An online search for local options should be a good starting point for exploring different styles, types of music and formats of classes. Ask if you can observe a class before committing to a whole term (see resources for examples of projects).

Cool Down (can also be used for warm-up)

Self-massage

Beginning with the hands, rub them together gently, covering all sides of the hands.

Imagine that you are washing your hands with soap, rubbing the backs, and in between the fingers.

Gently rub up one arm, all the way to the armpit.

Next rub the top of the chest, across the collarbone and sternum with both hands.

Move down and rub the bottom of the ribcage and the stomach, moving in circles around the stomach.

If possible, reach around to rub the kidneys on the back (you may need to lean forward to reach here).

Next, rub the thighs, around the knees and as far down the shins as you can reach. It is okay if you can only reach the top of your thighs or your knees.

If possible, lean forward, rub the tops of the feet, and then return up the backs of the legs, rubbing the calves.

Rub the face, moving the cheeks, opening the mouth to relax the jaw.

Then bring the fingers to the top of the head and tap as though raindrops are falling on the skull, moving around the head and down the cheeks. (Akādemi, 2017)

THINGS TO EXPERIENCE

- As performers:

Participatory community dance projects are also a meaningful way to engage in dance. The aim of such projects is to engage the general public in creating and performing dance with friends and families, and in diverse communities across the world. Below, we offer examples of ongoing projects in the UK which are aimed at different age and ability groups.

Young People Performing

The previous chapter described how the wide range of classes of Leeds dance company DAZL reduces children and young people's inequalities and inactivity. Performing dance is a key component of the DAZL model for championing positive achievement and bringing the community together. DAZL compares it to how football matches are to football training. Training classes prepare young people for performing their skills to an audience. They stage many local and large-scale showcases, performance opportunities and dance competition events each year. DAZL offers a positive outlook for disadvantaged communities where often the attention is on problems.

> *Championing the achievements of the children and young people encourages the families to invest not only time but positive engagement in these activities and build new relationships. This leads to support and volunteering at these events which enables DAZL to grow as an organisation and more effectively with the wider community. (Rodley, 2020, p. 3)*

Evaluative reporting of their projects and case studies has evidenced that the performative activities that DAZL organised – which can be performance but also celebrations or even sometimes competitions – are a fundamental contribution to the young people's wellbeing in a meaningful and sustainable way. Furthermore, the report demonstrates how young people's engagement with performance leads some of them to become active 'producers' of health and wellbeing (Rodley, 2020, p. 3).

Boys and Men Performing

ZoieLogic Dance Theatre works in education and community settings. The company has an acclaimed reputation 'for getting guys dancing' (ZoieLogic, 2021). At the centre of their work are their three youth companies which are all focusing on making boys and men dance. FuzzyVision is a fun and creative space for developing physical and creative expression for young boys (7–12). FuzzyLogic is a company for young males (12–18) who want to study dance at professional level. FuzzyClear is an all-male youth dance company for young lads with autism and other sensory differences. Following the company's successful creative projects supporting male mental health, the artistic director Zoie Golding is working on a large-scale performance for spring 2026 in Southampton (UK) with 100 male non-dancers dancing in solidarity to support men's mental health.

Performing Dance in Later Life

For 20 years, London-based venue Sadler's Wells' pioneering Company of Elders has offered people in later life a chance to dance and perform in the UK and internationally. Company members come from a range of different backgrounds; some may have danced when they were younger, and this is a chance to reconnect with that past experience. For others, dance is something they have taken up since retiring. The age range varies from 60+ to late 80s (Smith, 2018). The group is led by a rehearsal director and meets weekly to create new work with choreographers in a range of styles including contemporary, hip-hop and South Asian dance. The focus on performance gives a sense of purpose to the members. While the social aspect is important for participants, the aim and commitment that they are going to present something on stage make it especially more purposeful. For Sadler's Wells' Director of Learning and Engagement, Joce Giles, '[t]he presence that [an older performer] can bring to the stage has a different quality – and it is something that audiences find very powerful' (Smith, 2018).

Performing for Stroke Survivors

Stroke Odysseys investigates a performance arts model for neurological rehabilitation through the exploration of the potential of combining movement, song and performance. It is led by Rosetta Life, an art in health innovation charity, and delivered in partnership with stroke survivors in south London and five London NHS trusts. A series of performance workshops brings together people living with the effects of a stroke, researchers and clinicians. Initial discussions around questions about arts and neurorehabilitation, dance and the ethics of intimacy, music and rhythm and performance are incorporated into the production and design processes run by dancers and musicians in collaboration with the stroke survivors. Following the performance, Rosetta Life facilitates reflective practice conversations with the audiences (Jarrett, 2018). The evaluation of the project concluded that 'participants felt less isolated and lonely, regained "voice" and "power" and improved communication and relationships with people outside the "stroke community"' (Jarrett, 2018, p. 28). The collaboration extends into a tour around the UK to share these findings and to enable the performance itself to advocate effectively for life after stroke.

Look at our resources section to identify a performance group relevant to your community that you might be able to join. Using a simple search on the internet for 'community performance dance group' + relevant keywords (children, males, older people, disability, ...) might help to find appropriate local initiatives.

- As an observer:

We can learn to dance and about dance through observation. As I have discussed earlier, bodies have the capacity to imitate and synchronise movement, whether we are dancing or not. Audience members can feel an embodied engagement while watching dance as if they were experiencing movement sensations and related feelings and ideas. The more pleasure spectators feel while watching dance, the closer they engage in the process of performing the dance themselves (Reason & Reynolds, 2010). Become a dance audience member by watching recorded or live performances at festivals, in theatre spaces, at local venues or by engaging with dance television shows such as *Strictly Come Dancing* and international versions or full-length dance performances online such as Alvin Ailey Dance Theatre at Lincoln Centre.

Practice watching dance:

- Quietly sitting, observe people's movements, walks and gestures.
- Observe the dance of the natural environment (animals/trees, rivers ... how do natural shapes invite specific movement such as circles, lines, ...).
- When watching others dancing, pay attention to movements you recognise. This will allow an easier sense of interpretation. Look out for contrasting dynamics (stamping versus gliding across the space).
- Listening to the music while watching the dance allows another entry to meaningful emotional cues.

A dance does not always mean anything specific. Dance does not necessarily need to be understood. It is to be sensually experienced. It might provoke questions, reflections or invite you to unknown places in your imagination and in your body.

SUMMARY

This chapter has offered a wide range of tasks, strategies and ideas for you to engage with dancing in your life. Whether you are trying these exercises at home, online or outdoors; on your own, in a group or with a partner – regardless of your environment, or abilities, whether you have never danced or you are already an accomplished dancer, we hope that the activities introduced here will inspire you to explore further how dance can benefit you and your family. This section shows that there are many degrees of engagement with dancing – from an active social participation to a more personal and reflective process; whether you only have 10 min or you want to engage in a longer-term project, dancing offers a meaningful and transformative way to overcome some of our perceived limitations.

We continue to explore the positive physical, mental, and social outcomes of dancing by outlining the dynamic relationships between vital human physiological and sensory functions such as memory, coordination, synchrony and touch and specific dance principles such as rhythms, partnering and the use of images, objects and improvisation. More importantly, the activities described are offered as a starting point for dancing. All the tasks can be adapted to your own body and environment. There is no need for a special dance floor or expensive dance gear, but safety is the first requirement. Awareness of our own needs as well as the needs of other dancing participants is key to healthy practice. Careful judgement is required to negotiate the balance between building confidence in moving and over-stretching our limits. Input from professional dance artists is key to developing your dancing. We recommend reading this chapter in conjunction with the resources section (Chapter 7) which signposts a range of classes (in-person and online).

5

WHAT CAN PROFESSIONALS DO TO HELP?

There are a range of dance for health activities taking place across the UK and internationally that support more traditional, medical strategies to maintaining or improving health and wellbeing. This chapter offers examples of dance and creative movement activities being delivered by dance artists in different healthcare contexts including care homes and primary care. A brief introduction of each setting precedes specific approaches to remind the reader of their characteristics. The following case studies have been selected for their longstanding cooperation between dance and health professionals. These accounts of practices give a flavour of what is possible when these collaborative endeavours are successful. The writing of these case studies is reflective and includes participants' responses to the range of activities presented. These insights further demonstrate the benefits of creative dance approaches for health and wellbeing as a result of collaborative person-centred care. There are also detailed descriptions of specific techniques that are intended to inspire professionals to start using dance and creative movement principles in their own approach to health.

It is very important that dance provision is delivered by a qualified and experienced dance artist/practitioner, to ensure that dance activity is safe, appropriate and of good quality. This section offers some ideas on how to collaborate with dance artists, as well as information for health and dance professionals that want to train further in dancing for health.

SOCIAL CARE HOMES

The methodological challenges of researching dancing in care homes have limited the rigour of findings on the efficacy of dancing in care homes. However, when the conditions are right, dance can be an engaging activity for older people living in care (Guzmán-García et al., 2013). The diverse range of physical and cognitive abilities found among care home residents and the lack of funding can be a challenge to dance interventions, but, with a supportive team of staff and experienced dance artists, many projects have been successful (Gomaa et al., 2020). In particular, studies have evidenced how creative participatory activities, including dance, have a positive impact in promoting social relationships for older people within care homes (Dadswell et al., 2020).

Dance activities in care homes range from Parkinson's focused creative projects to physical exercise classes. Other initiatives are bringing dancers together with practitioners of other art forms to create an interdisciplinary experience for the participants, harnessing the value of combining dance with activities such as music, drama or fine art. Dance companies such as Green Candle Dance, which has been engaging care home residents with dance for over 20 years, have evaluated the impact of their work. They have found that 'the participants showed evidence of improved wellbeing and positive moods, better co-ordination and sequencing, demonstrations of being in the here-and-now, positive social interactions and greater confidence, a reduction of listlessness and distress, and enhanced relationships with carers' (Green Candle Dance, 2016).

We draw below on a useful dancing toolkit from projects that have taken place in care home settings across Cornwall (AFHC, 2010). The toolkit includes ideas, advice and inspiration to begin your own dance sessions in a care setting. There is practical information to take into consideration when running dance sessions in care settings relating to choice of location, the length of sessions and the use of props, music and other support. You will find a link to download the toolkit in the resource section (Chapter 7).

Most dancing in care settings is carried out while sitting, but when it can be done safely, there are opportunities to get up and dance for those who are able to. Such sessions are designed to facilitate working with groups of people; however, they can easily be adapted for one-to-one activity. I have selected a specific theme below to summarise one of the approaches included in the toolkit.

Setting Up Tea Chair Dance Sessions

These sessions are aimed at older people, their relatives and friends as an invitation to tea dancing. It does need a little explanation so that people understand that they don't have to be standing up for the dancing to happen. People can stay seated or, if they wish, they can be assisted in their dancing by another person.

Theme: Tango; Music: Tango music; Time: 30–45 min

Props: Tango dance photographs/colourful scarves/hats/fabric cloths/instruments (shakers, tambourines,. ...)

(1) *Introducing the theme*: what do participants know about tango, its origins and characteristics (music, clothing, ...)

(2) *Warm-up*: (imagine we wake up and find ourselves in hot South America!)

- Close your eyes, take a few deep breaths.
- Bring hands to face and rub gently, slowly stretch out arms to shoulder height and yawn, repeat this a few times to stretch and wake up the body.
- Hold arms out in front of you, and flex hands up and down, then side to side, then introduce head turning with movement.
- Close and open hands and fingers with 'sunshine hands' and palms facing away from the body.
- Rub up and down arms and into legs (imagine: 'putting sun cream on').
- Draw toes and feet up, then stretch and relax flat (imagine: 'sand between toes').

- Start a gentle walking, jogging, into water and splashing with both feet (imagine: 'walking on the beach').
- Make diving action lifting arms and head then diving forwards, open arms to side (imagine: 'diving into the sea'). Repeat three or four times.
- Rest (imagine: lying on the beach, taking in the sun), breathing deeply from the abdomen.

(3) Creative section

- Hand out props, show tango photographs, talk about the tango dance and how the props make them feel in relation to the dance.
- Ask individual participants to find a simple movement related to a prop or item of clothing. Support and encourage their ideas.
- Ask the group to try the movement out too.
- Using the movements create a sequence, put this to the music, and have the group try it out together.

(4) *Tango sequence*: emphasise this is a proud dance with the body lifted, and head held high.

- Start with clapping, elbows lifted out to sides (×8).
- Two slow claps then three quick.
- Repeat above with feet joining in stamping (while sitting or standing).
- Using arms only take tango ballroom hold (left bent in, right extended), head turned in direction of extended arm. Change direction of arms with head (×4).
- With arms still in ballroom hold and legs fairly close together (or parallel), introduce leg work, right leg steps away from body to right side, left leg follows with step to right side of body also. Step left leg back to original position,

right follows back to original position. Change arms and repeat other side (×4).

- Perform together both the group's sequence and the taught sequence together with music.

(5) Cool-down

- Imagine lying on a beach, looking up at the stars, with warm sand enveloping the body.
- Stretch each limb out, stretch the whole body, and yawn as in the warm-up but slower.
- Feel seawater lapping at the feet; gently flex feet up and down.
- Focus on breathing deeply and evenly.
- Enjoy listening to music, relax and rest.

PRIMARY CARE, HOSPITALS OR OTHER CLINICS

For many years now, dance has been a part of primary care provision in medicalised settings. Often offered as a creative alternative to – or in support of – traditional physiotherapy, dance can get people moving and rehabilitating without conscious effort. It can also foster creative and playful atmospheres in clinical settings which can sometimes feel frightening or sterile. As previously mentioned, Dance Movement Psychotherapy is a recognised form of treatment and can offer an alternative to traditional therapies within primary care.

Research has evidenced the significant benefits of dance interventions in hospitals for patients, staff and families. Patients have been found to experience an enhancement to their physical, emotional and social wellbeing. They value the opportunity to interact with others in a 'non-medical' context. Dance offers a temporary escape from the medical environment and the opportunity to be relieved from boredom. The adverse effect of prolonged immobilisation of inpatients is a well-known issue within traditional acute hospitals – and is sometimes referred to as a deconditioning process coined 'pyjama paralysis'. Staying in pyjamas longer than needed reinforces the 'sick role' for patients; they lose their mobility and their risk of infection increases. 'Pyjama paralysis' can slow the process of recovery (Cummings, 2017). Deconditioning is a major contributor to falls in older adults (Fitzpatrick et al., 2019). Dance can be effective in fighting pyjama paralysis. Indeed, the NHS estimates that a 70-day national campaign launched by England's chief nursing officer prevented patients from spending an extra 710,000 days in hospital (2018). It offers a fun way to alleviate the impact of isolation and inactivity and provides an opportunity to socialise with others on the ward, including staff members.

Inclusive and flexible approaches are used by professional dance and movement artists to ensure that the activity is accessible and beneficial to patients with a wide range of abilities and needs. Although not therapists, dance artists are increasingly integrated within multidisciplinary teams working along occupational therapists, physiotherapists and speech and language therapists, particularly where treatment is for older people or involves physical rehabilitation or neurological conditions.

DANCE FOR HEALTH IN HOSPITAL – OLDER PATIENTS

Dance for Health is Cambridge University Hospitals' (CUH) flagship arts programme which has become an international leader in the field of participatory dance within hospital settings. Described as a non-clinical creative health practice, it is one of the UK's longest running hospital dance initiatives. Since it was established in 2014, the programme has engaged with over 5,000 people with a wide range of abilities and needs.

Filipa Pereira-Stubbs is the lead dance artist who created the position at CUH, devised a range of sessions for multiple wards and has been developing the scheme for 10 years, working collaboratively with health professionals and clinical ward staff. She delivers regular weekly interventions embedded on eight different wards including the elderly, stroke rehabilitation, paediatrics, diabetes and endocrinology wards.

Pereira-Stubbs devised creative movement sessions that address the multifaceted needs of patients in a way that is also accessible to medical staff. The sessions can take place in beds, chairs, wheelchairs or anywhere that patients can be made to feel comfortable and in control of their own movement. As Pereira-Stubbs (2024) states:

> *There is no expectation or desired outcome outlined by the dance artist. By focusing on the positive potential of how we want to move, side stepping assessment of what's wrong, we open ourselves to the wisdom of the body-mind connection and our body's innate ability to heal.*

Although not therapy, the sessions are often of therapeutic value by improving the hospital experience for inpatients so that they can regain their confidence, overall wellbeing and physical strength, and avoid readmission to hospital. Pereira-Stubbs' approach offers a bridge between medicalised perspectives on the body and a wider somatic approach. She combines anatomical information, movement improvisation and imagination to accommodate differences between patients such as health conditions, age and culture.

In a collective session, during what Pereira-Stubbs terms *anatomical warm-up improvisation*, she will map physiological abilities in the group, reassuring people as to their ability and inviting people to relax, to engage and to express themselves in their own way. Patients return to a sense of themselves when they move in this expressive, personal way. The focus of the movement is on finding who and how the person is and what they are bringing to their hospital experience. Describing her approach, in mapping both the group and the individuals, Pereira-Stubbs (2024) speaks of:

> *Doing symmetrical stretching out movements, checking the proprioception, looking up right left and down, all done in a way that does not look like an exercise; releasing the shoulder, opening the lungs, singing and then the energy comes back, the connections, spirit, the emotions follow, that is what dance does.*

Pereira-Stubbs' approach to dance is not just about exercise. In these clinical, goal-focused wards, dance is an invitation to engage with others through a creative process that often becomes joyous. Dance becomes fun, and a space for storytelling and self-expression. Using music, imagination and positive physiological information, she invites people to express who they are or who they have been.

Patients who work with Pereira-Stubbs benefit from an increased sense of agency through self-expression. Often hospitalised people have a limited say over what is happening to them next, or lack a sense of agency over their choice of treatment or medication. According to Pereira-Stubbs, creative dance movement allows people to restore a sense of themselves, and as part of a programme of treatment, developing a sense of integrity, will and agency can also help people become better. Dance offers something different in a medical environment. The nature of the engagement in a session is different because the dance artist listens to the whole person and helps the patient make connections with oneself and others. Each session may bring hope, integrity and expressivity.

Sessions also focus on bringing relaxation, comfort or joy to patients. The combination of music, calm movement or singing while dancing releases positive chemicals. People are smiling and some anxieties may fade. They begin to share stories. They start to express themselves. In one of Pereira Stubbs' sessions on a DME (Department of Medicine for the Elderly) ward, a small group of women realised that some of them had been to school together, and furthermore, they recognised a blind man from their youth. They shared with the rest of the group that he had been a skilled tap dancer. Through the warmup and the exercises, and with the support of the staff, he started to tap dance. Pereira-Stubbs (2024) describes a special moment in her teaching:

> *We were afraid that he might be falling or something, but he had an absolute muscle memory and at the end of the session everybody was laughing, it was so joyous, a very special standout moment with the staff too. Nobody was ill in that room.*

This kind of improvisational movement dance approach works well in a hospital environment as sessions can take place anywhere. Moreover, the approach does not rely on teaching steps or dance-based exercises. The point is not to deliver a dancing lesson. A body, a pulse ... that is all we need to make a positive change.

Even for those people that have significant difficulty with movement, patterns of breathing can shift, muscles can relax and Pereira-Stubbs may see a change of emotion, moving through tears to laughs. During one-to-one sessions, the offer to move is still based on metaphors, images and often language. For example, someone's hand might be inflamed, very painful or hot. Imagining that the hand rests in cool water and exploring how that might feel, while introducing movement, can be a soothing embodied experience for a patient with limited movement.

The use of imagination helps the patient step out of self-imposed boundaries which are often there because of shock, pain, trauma or confusion. Pereira-Stubbs observes that people in these conditions can sometimes pull back and stay stuck. Helping people to relax and find more ease is the first step. This might be achieved by adjusting pillows, making eye contact, quiet words and listening, with hands quietly and gently restoring connection with the body, taking them to a place where they can move a bit more freely and begin to engage. The next step, which is about communicating positive physiological information, can then begin:

> *If you are bringing your hand above the heart level, you are helping the heart muscle to pump. If you uncurl your hand, you are shifting your elbow, you are then shifting your shoulder, then the ribcage is then opening your lung ... you can breathe more easily ... (Pereira-Stubbs, 2024)*

While working with dance principles, dance artists such as Pereira-Stubbs use a careful choice of familiar language to offer an individualised rehabilitating process which engages with the quality of the inpatient's life, bringing connections and joy.

DANCE AS PART OF A MULTIDISCIPLINARY APPROACH TO PAIN MANAGEMENT FOR BABIES AND CHILDREN IN HOSPITAL

Small Things Dance Collective (STDC) has been collaborating with the Alder Hey Children's Hospital in Liverpool for over 17 years.

The work of the artistic director, Lisa Dowler, in improvisational, somatic and environmental dance practices has been embedded into the hospital through bedside one-to-one sessions with babies, children and young people on the cardiac and neurorehabilitation wards. Another strand of the company is their performance work which takes place in public spaces in the hospital, or as one-to-one bespoke performances in children's bedrooms. Since the COVID-19 pandemic in 2020, the company has also produced socially distanced performance projects for children including film projections, and immersive or VR experiences. Thus, the collective offers weekly artists' sessions weaved with performance creative works.

The work of STDC with children and young people is based on a non-verbal approach to communication which is a key skill in dance. More specifically, Dowler uses her skills in contact improvisation in a range of subtle ways to relate to the young patients. For example, these might include observing small changes in a person's expression, gestures or physiology, then following and responding to these changes. Skills also include making contact with the child by applying what Dowler names *a listening touch*. Drawing on her training in Body-Mind Centering® (BMC®), she explains that this 'quality of touch has the same intention as an invitation: it is a listening, non-directive touch, it is a "being with" rather than a "doing to" touch' (Dowler, 2016, p. 22). This quality of touch is captured in Fig. 9.

Dowler does not always feel it is appropriate to describe herself as a dancer, as the public may have specific perceptions of dance. And parents may sometimes think that their child's illness prevents them from dancing. Dowler introduces her practice as a creative and sensory movement activity:

> *I am thinking about shifting in the body that could be shifting from a tense state to a relaxed state that is movement to me. Once people have seen or experienced a session, what it can do for the children then they often ask for more, saying, 'Can you come back tomorrow?' (L. Dowler, personal communication, 2024)*

The collaboration between dance artists and health professionals is crucial when working in children's hospitals. To develop a

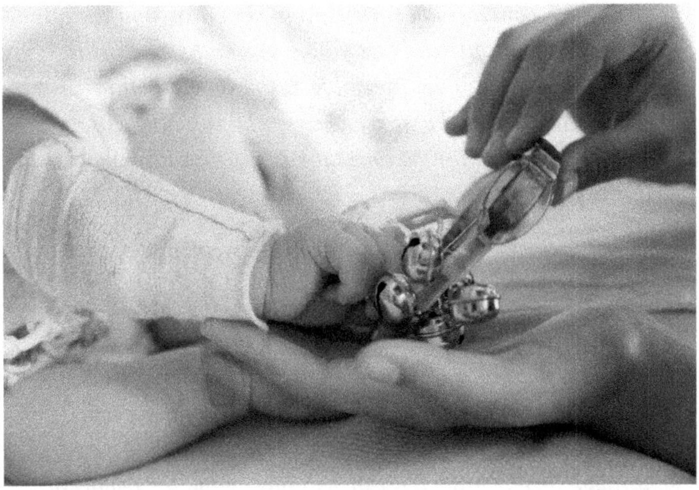

Source: Photo credit: Leila Romaya.

Fig. 9. Small Things Dance Artist Exploring Movement and Touch with a Baby on the Cardiac Unit of Alder Hey Children's Hospital.

sense of cooperation and mutual understanding of each other's approaches, Dowler has developed strategies to find ways to articulate to health professionals the various crossovers between somatic dance improvisation practice and health practices. For example, the study of Developmental Movement Patterns is central to the BMC® method and is also key in neurophysiotherapy for helping repatterning processes after brain injuries.

Individual bedside sessions:

In her article, 'Can improvised somatic dance reduce acute pain for young people in hospital?', Dowler (2016) explains the one-to-one bedside somatic dance session in three stages. The first stage is defined as the meeting place:

> *The practitioner enters the space quietly and slowly, introducing themselves following the timing of the child or young person. The practitioner becomes aware of their own breathing and rhythm and attempts to tune into and match that of the child or young person. They have a calm energetic state and make themselves smaller by crouching, and less imposing by softening their gaze rather than*

direct eye contact. They wait for a verbal or non-verbal invitation from the child or young person to move closer, sometimes using a sensory object, toy or musical instrument to mediate the space. For children with ABI the practitioner might introduce themselves through touch as a way of communication.

The second stage is a duet of creative movement exploration.

This includes the subtle movement of the breath to a more physical and expansive moving through space. This is about sharing a dance, and collaborating and deciding nonverbally – moment to moment – what that dance will be. This includes playing with sensory objects, creating a story through imagination, but can also stay within the realms of barely perceptible or micro dances, such as small shifts in muscular tone, quality of movement and relationship.

The final stage offers rest and relaxation, which may be '... achieved by using objects such as feathers and balloons with a soft quality or restful touch, rolling body balls or drawing' (Dowler, 2016, p. 22).

Dowler's movement and dance work with young people in hospitals contributes to the development of a patient-centred approach to health care whereby the value of personal experience and creativity is at the centre of the care and recovery process. Global models of healthcare design have been shifting towards more multidimensional ways of treating patients. This is reflected in the growing popularisation of the concept of collaborative health and the development of worldwide social prescribing schemes. Paying attention to questions of how best to establish a collaborative relationship with the people we are working with is very important for professionals seeking to develop integrated care through dance and creative movement.

PRIMARY CARE: GENERAL PRACTICE

[T]he idea of a doctor as a teacher – or maybe a sharer of information would be better – to help people be able to

> *make decisions. I think there is an increasing desire not to be the passive recipient of medicine. [Dr Gavin Young, GP – Extract from interview with dance artist Miranda Tufnell (Tufnell, 2017, p. 9)]*

In the UK, national surveys reveal to us that over 40% of people want to be more involved in decisions about their care, and similarly 40% of people living with long-term conditions want more support to manage their health and wellbeing on a day-to-day basis (NHS, 2017). These findings require holistic models of staffing for general practices (GPs) which can foster innovative and creative collaborations. Local practices are slowly shifting away from having only a team of nurses and GPs towards employing a greater range of healthcare staff including social prescribing link workers, and physiotherapists who can work in collaboration with dance artists. With an expanded team, medical centres can offer more personalised care by developing more knowledge and awareness of local resources available for patients. Many of the dance activities and case studies that we have outlined in this book can make a significant contribution to this shift in primary care settings from symptom-led care to 'whole person' health care. Dance and creative movement practices as a complementary medicine can help GP practices by supporting and enhancing healthy living. This has been evidenced by the early results of the evaluation of the recent social prescribing scheme (National Academy for Social Prescribing, 2024) which we further discuss in Chapter 6.

ESTABLISHING A GROUP

Miranda Tufnell worked as an Alexander technique teacher and dance artist at the Temple Sowerby Medical Centre near Penrith in rural Cumbria for 14 years. In her beautiful book, *When I Open My Eyes* (2017), Tufnell offers several accounts of creative projects and practices that grew out of her creative and therapeutic practice in a GP surgery. She describes with detail 'the palette of possibilities' that have been developed in collaboration with patients. She shares the responses of participants including patients, carers, nurses and doctors to the creative activities.

Tufnell's account of these projects highlights the delicate process of establishing a group. She reminds us that illness often creates a sense of isolation which undermines people's sense of agency and purpose in life. Personal histories can create apprehension around the idea of joining a group. The collective process can be overwhelming, and it is, therefore, important to take time to understand peoples' interests, concerns and needs. Yet the sense of security and trust that is experienced when participation is skilfully facilitated is important for the health, wellbeing and recovery of patients. For Tufnell, 'A group becomes a kind of family, where people feel at ease and comfortable together' (Tufnell, 2017, p. 13).

> *On our first day, Tim [my collaborator] and I brought branches of richly coloured autumn leaves, which we set in a glass vase in a window to catch the sun, alongside a bowl of fruit. This made a rather dowdy village hall feel more hospitable [...] We began sitting in a circle and introduced ourselves with observations about the weather and inquiries about where people had come from asking each person what they would most like help with from the sessions. All spoke in different ways of their stiffness, coldness and pain in moving. Even in that first meeting, others responded and offered suggestions, which made a warm and friendly start. (Tufnell, 2017, p. 14)*

This sense of care in establishing a group echoes many of the experiences voiced by dance artists in this book. For example, Sandra Golding's earlier perspectives (Chapter 3) on the importance of taking time to create relationships in her African Caribbean community dance workshops reminded us that trust is a first step towards healthier communities.

It is essential that you as a professional feel confident that you can create the conditions for mutual trust within the groups that you are working with. Further training might be required to strengthen your skills in building a safe space for your patients. Below are practical accounts of training which focus on developing movement-based creative strategies to care for your patients as well as for yourselves.

TRAINING

For Health Professionals

Transforming the Doctor–Patient Relationship – Stuart Pimsler Dance and Theatre (USA)

Stuart Pimsler Dance and Theatre (SPDT) (2023) company has been at the forefront of arts and health for three decades. Pimsler and company co-artistic director Suzanne Costello have created performances and residencies for caregivers in professional settings and in homes. They delivered workshops in colleges and universities, hospitals, hospices and social service organisations in the USA and abroad. They have focused on keeping care givers healthy and on developing creative strategies to invigorate the practices of health professionals and of artists who are interested in collaborating with the healthcare community.

Empathy and an inclination to help others is the initial motivation of caregivers and health professionals. However, over time, stress and exhaustion can sometimes prevent individuals from offering the care that they anticipated at the beginning of their career. Drawing on their many conversations with doctors and health professionals over their career, Pimsler and Costello came to understand that the medical context itself was one of the main challenges for developing high quality care for patients. The demands of training and other workplace conditions can place significant restrictions on the time available for caregivers to care for patients or to dedicate to their own self-care. The emphasis on an arguably narrow range of scientific facts during training can undermine the relational aspect of the practice, while the transition between the classroom and the hectic environment of the hospital is often highly challenging for new health professionals. In addition, the traumatic aspects of professional health work can sometimes mark the caregiver's day-to-day life. Compassion fatigue is another common side effect of caregiving work (Garnett et al., 2023). For Costello and Pimsler, a decline of empathy can be understood with reference to a number of exacerbating factors including a lack of role models, the volume of on-the-job learning required, time pressures as well as operating in an environment with strains sometimes stemming from hierarchical structures and bureaucracy.

In their programme named *Transforming the Doctor–Patient Relationship*, Pimsler and Costello focus on responding to the professional caregiver's need to develop more personal awareness of how to interact with those seeking their advice and care (Fig. 10). Delivered as a series of workshops, the sessions use dance principles – such as synchronisation and touch – to engage caregivers in creative expression. It introduces them to self-reflective embodied relational techniques which might include, for example, movement, voice, writing or drawing. Workshop participants start by recovering their inspiration for becoming a caregiver and, thus, reframe key principles of their practices. One keen workshop participant shared his surprise to have discovered through engaging with the exercises in the workshop, 'how relational the practice of medicine is' (Pimsler, 2021, p. 33).

In the summer of 2023, Costello was invited to facilitate a series of workshops entitled *Caring for the Caregiver* at the Mayo Clinic

Source: Photo credit: Courtesy of the artist.

Fig. 10. Transforming the Doctor–Patient Relationship Workshop Participant.

in Rochester, USA. The workshops use the creation of movement stories and active listening techniques to reconnect health professionals with their initial call for caring and medical professions. Costello outlines the structure and content of the workshop below:

> *After introductions, participants are led through a series of easy stretching exercises while seated. Then they are asked to close their eyes and recall one memory associated with the prompt: 'The first time I remember being cared for…'. They are encouraged to remember all the sensory parts of this memory – smells, sounds, visual elements, tastes and feelings. Using writing, movement and active listening, participants are invited to work in pairs to create movement stories which are performed to the rest of the group to inform a reflective peer discussion. (S. Costello, personal communication, 2024)*

The focus on the sensorial aspect of communication found in Pimsler and Costello's approach points to a new way for health professionals to relate to people in their practice. As one of the workshop participants shares below, the exploration of interpersonal relationships through creative dance movement can help develop a higher sense of empathy in therapeutic relations:

> *The workshop is an exercise in a dimension that is not often entered for scientifically inclined people for a variety of unclear reasons; however, if one pays attention, it is an essential component of being and listening. It is a way of being empathic; of listening, of caring and ultimately healing. (Mayo Clinic Physician in S. Costello, personal communication, 2024)*

Partner work can be particularly helpful for caregivers as they are constantly in a collaborative duet with their patients and 'duet exercises allow participants to challenge and deepen their individual boundaries of relational intimacy' (Pimsler, 2010, p. 62). Both exercises below start with a partner.

Landscapes: practising observational skills

This exercise highlights the importance of really seeing the patient before acting. Pimsler and Costello note that 'it is difficult for caregivers because their personalities, education and workplaces often stress immediate action' (Pimsler, 2010, p. 67).

In pairs (A/B), then progress in a larger group.

> *A assumes a still shape.*
>
> *B observes A.*
>
> *B complements their partner's shape – considering negative space (the empty space surrounding A); and positive space (their partner's body); the feeling evoked by the still shape and deciding whether physical contact might occur.*
>
> *After the duet-landscape is formed, A leaves the stillness and observes B, and then decides on a new shape.*

This creates a sequence which alternates between observing, moving and stillness. As the group becomes larger, decision making becomes more complicated, and participants need to keep track of when it is their turn!

Practising letting go, holding on or helping: A closes their eyes and trusts B to guide them through the room.

> *B looks at A and considers their partner as a living sculpture (considering their physical characteristics).*
>
> *B moves selected body parts of A (hands, arms, head).*
>
> *B escorts A through the space.*
>
> *A keeps their eyes closed the entire time and allows their partner to take care of them.*
>
> *Swap roles so that each partner experiences being both caregiver and care receiver.*

During this practice, Pimsler and Costello invite A to apply clear nonverbal signals that welcome the weighted release of their partner's limbs and head. Similarly, they ask B to reflect on which parts of their body they are able to release – yielding to another.

Reflective practice for participants:

- What was your experience of having your head held?
- Were you able to let your head be held by another, feeling its weight in your partner's hand? (letting go)
- What did you experience/feel if you were not able to release your head to your partner? (holding on)
- Did you try to help your partner by assisting them in moving your own head? (helping)

This exercise can become a highlight of the workshop series. In the words of one workshop participant, it helped 'shaking off the notion that "touch is unprofessional"' (Pimsler, 2021, p. 76).

For Pimsler and Costello, we should care about what doctors feel because the health of caregivers affects their healing skills. Drawing on the American choreographer and dancer Anna Halprin's personal experience of healing through movement, they advocate the benefits for health professionals to creatively explore the emotional connectivity between body and mind. That intersection is the centre from which a new doctor–patient relationship can emerge. The work of Stuart Pimsler Dance and Theatre helps health professionals recognise the healing power of person-to-person relationships involved in health care. Their approach to collaborative health can be described as a movement of emancipation on both sides of the relationship: through reclaiming the permission to move and touch, caregivers can support and encourage patients to be more in control of their own health. In the UK, shared responsibility for health and the development of a personal care model features as part of the objectives of the NHS's long-term plan to enhance people's involvement in their own health care. The intention is to give 'people more control over their own health and the care they receive, encourage more collaboration between GPs, their teams and community services, as "primary care networks"' (NHS, 2019).

For Dance Professionals

Dancers working in a health context often express a rewarding sense of purposefulness through their practice. As artists, dancers have acquired skills over time that give them unique opportunities to give back to communities in need. However, it is important to develop the specific skills and knowledge required to work in participatory settings. Such settings often involve working with very vulnerable individuals and in cooperation with other caregivers. Care homes and hospitals are obviously often very busy places, and it requires time and experience to deliver dance activities safely and successfully in these working conditions.

Even if you already have the necessary qualifications, it is important to continue developing your skills and your networks to continue supporting your practice. Dance artists and practitioners working on the ground can often feel isolated in their own local environment. Having regular continuing professional development input is a good way of not only connecting with others working in specific areas of practice but also keeping up to date with new opportunities and developments.

There are a range of international training and development opportunities for professional dancers including in-person and online courses. In the UK, the national organisation *People Dancing* offers professional qualifications, online courses and networks which include e-newsletters, online resources, events and gatherings (People Dancing, 2024). I introduce below the international training *Dance Health Alliance*™ based in Australia in order to offer further insights into what to expect if you want to train to deliver dance in health settings.

Training for Dance Enthusiasts: Dance Health Alliance™ (Australia)

Dance Health Alliance™ (DHA) is a non-profit organisation that creates special dance programmes to help people with mobility issues, cognitive diseases and mental health challenges, and older adults. These programmes aim to improve quality of life, restore balance between body and mind and fight against illness.

DHA offers distinct training workshops for health and care professionals as well as for dancers, dance teachers and dance studio owners interested in implementing these programmes within their communities. Online training is also delivered in order to increase accessibility for people based in rural communities or overseas.

For Korebrits, CEO and Co-founder of DHA, dancing can be 'simply walking with style' (personal communication, 2024). The group's training emphasises the importance of making movements achievable. DHA's trainees learn how to facilitate seated dance movement sessions (as represented in Fig. 11) for a range of abilities, involving transitions from sitting to standing and moving, the use of chairs as a balance tool, the use of music and rhythm, movement games, basic choreography and improvisation.

The training often attracts ex-dancers who have moved to the healthcare sector and perhaps miss their days of being able to express themselves through their body. Korebrits often receives feedback from participants thanking her for being allowed to dance again – 'I thought my dancing days were over!' For Korebrits, 'it's a beautiful gift to reignite trainees' and participants' spark for their passion for dance' (personal communication, 2024).

Engaging in DHA dance sessions stimulates cognitive processes. The combination of music and movement elements in the dance class can help people recollect past experiences. Korebrits refers to

Source: Photo credit: Joshuajamesfilm.

Fig. 11. DHA DanceWise Programme in Action NoosaCare – Carramar Queensland.

the privilege of witnessing people living with dementia becoming more present as memories flow back: 'I have often had conversations with people whom later I have been told had not spoken for months' (personal communication, 2024).

Mary, one frail elderly woman in a wheelchair with advanced dementia, who had not spoken for weeks, surprised her carers when, during a session, her head lifted and her eyes gained a spark; she started clapping and moving her feet to the music. The classic war song began to play, 'Wish Me Luck as You Wave Me Goodbye'. She started to sing at the top of her voice and to march her legs in time to the music. Mary told the movement practitioner of her husband, an Australian soldier. She spoke warmly of her children, naming them all and how they continued to look after her, physically and financially, visiting regularly. According to Korebrits, the impact of the music and movement stimulated her memory pathways to help her reminisce about past experiences. The movement practitioner felt honoured to have witnessed such exceptional coherent behaviour (G. Korebrits, personal communication, 2024).

SUMMARY

This chapter offered some examples of how to use creative and dance principles in several health settings and with a range of participants including older people, babies and children. It requires practice and experience to work effectively using each of the approaches discussed here, particularly when taking into account the target populations. The aim of this section was to give an insight into longstanding and successful collaborations between members of health, social and community care workers and dance artists. It outlined the skills and qualities required, as well as offering some techniques to develop these qualities in a professional practice. The latter part of the chapter outlined two examples of training for health and dance professionals who want to further train in dancing for health. Training is one of the areas identified as in need of improvement for the development of creative health in the UK. The All-Party Parliamentary Group on Arts, Health and Wellbeing Report, *Creative Health: The Arts for Health and Wellbeing*, which was publicly launched at King's College in London in 2023, recommends further professional development for the education of clinicians, public health specialists and other health and care professionals. Based on our international case studies, it is clear this is something also needed outside of the UK. The report highlights the need for more arts courses which would be dedicated to the contribution of the arts to health and wellbeing (AfHW APPG, 2017, p. 10). Our next chapter will further focus on the potential challenges for dancing for health and how to overcome them.

6

HOW CAN WE ADDRESS CHALLENGES AND EMBRACE OPPORTUNITIES IN DANCING FOR HEALTH?

So, thus far, we have explored why dancing is valuable for our health and wellbeing, who dancing can and should be accessible to, ways in which you can dance and how professionals can collaboratively deliver and develop dancing for health initiatives. This chapter will now deal with the potential challenges dancing presents for the general public, health and wellbeing professionals as well as dance practitioners. These challenges are very present and felt for some people and shouldn't be underestimated. Therefore, we will also explore recommendations on how to overcome these barriers to a life in dancing. Many of these issues have been raised or addressed in earlier chapters of this book, and certainly in the case studies, as people have reflected on the journey of delivering and experiencing dance in different health contexts. This chapter will critically consider ways to overcome barriers by providing an overview of promoting factors or opportunities in applying dance and draw upon further case studies that demonstrate ways in which dancing for health and wellbeing is evolving and innovating to attend to the developing needs of the population and the advancements of modern society.

INCREASED AWARENESS TO INCREASED PARTICIPATION

There's a reason the popular saying is 'Dance like nobody's watching', rather than 'Dance like everybody's watching'. Dance can be daunting. The emphasis on the moving body, the perpetuated stereotypes of 'the dancer' and the vulnerability of an expressive and physical arts practice can make people feel actively excluded or wary of dance as an activity. Every year on the hit UK television show *Strictly Come Dancing*, at least one celebrity who is new to dance claims that they cannot dance or explains how scared they are about learning to dance. Dance can make us vulnerable. What nearly all, if not all, participants on *Strictly Come Dancing* say at the end of the programme is how much they love dance, how much they gained from it and how they will continue to dance long after the show. Dance can be transformative, but it is not always understood.

Developing understanding of how dance can impact people is important for increasing participation. There are excellent initiatives that have been launched to promote the benefits of dance, such as the Imperial Society of Teachers of Dancing's (ISTD) 'Find your Dance Space' campaign, which attempts to highlight the myriad of ways people can get involved in dance, and also the benefits of it (ISTD, 2024). As outlined in the introductory chapter, dance can be many things to many different people. Finding what dance provision is available in your local area, as well as what style interests and engages you as an individual, is important.

One of the main barriers to participation in dance is self-doubt. Dance for some people may have connotations of judgement, criticism and competition, as these are features of some genres or platforms for dancing. For example, ballroom competitions or ballet examinations have an emphasis on competitiveness and critique, while some dance styles such as Indian classical dance have a strict discipline central to mastery of the technique. Unpacking past experiences of dance can be challenging. There has been much action to develop approaches to dance for health and to address concerns around safeguarding and general practice that pays greater attention to the wellbeing of dancers. Dancing at different stages of life also brings new opportunities for growth and being in relation with dance.

Dancing for health resists the notion that dance is a form of activity that must be performed in a singular, normative way, with perfect aesthetic execution. Emphasising that there are different levels of dance activity, from chair dance classes to pre-professional training programmes, means that anyone can participate in dance activity, regardless of your fitness or physical performance level. Knowing your own body and your own limits is key to not only finding the right sessions but also for keeping yourself safe and well within the dance environment.

Dance does not have to take place only within a dedicated dance class. Dancing can occur anywhere! Tapping down the supermarket aisle or boogying while doing the washing up means that you don't have to be constrained by time pressure or being near a particular environment. For those living in rural areas, online dance classes can provide access to dancing for health opportunities. Offerings in Chapter 4 provide a way to engage with dancing from your own home, which is vital for those who might be bed bound or unable to leave their house, but can also benefit those who are simply reluctant to attend group classes, for whatever reason.

BROADENING ACCESS TO DANCE

As explored in Chapter 3, perceptions about who can dance, informed by stereotypes related to gender norms, social class, culture, religion and body type, can affect levels of engagement and participation in dance but also access to it. Dance should be accessible to everyone. While that doesn't mean that everyone will participate in dance by choice, everyone should have the opportunity to make that decision for themselves and have autonomy in their health and/or care experience (Sandman et al., 2012). Dance can also help develop the confidence to advocate yourself for your own health concerns and care plans.

One of the key access barriers to dance is the financial burden. Dance, as with many arts disciplines, has a perceived history of elitism and domination by the middle and upper social classes (Sanderson, 2008). Often this was due to the price of attending the theatre, but private dance classes also cost money. Of course, dance practitioners and educators should be rightly paid for their work and their expertise. There are some initiatives that are helping to ensure that dance practitioners are appropriately compensated and that classes are inclusive and accessible to those who might not otherwise be able to pay for dance sessions. Certain organisations offer pay-what-you-can or reduced fees for classes. Additionally, there are a range of subsidised dance activity sessions, toolkits and guides which mean that you don't always have to pay to participate.

Dance classes are also being prescribed by doctors, through social prescribing schemes or similar initiatives across the world (as mentioned in Chapters 2 and 5). This person-centred approach to healthcare treatment planning can, depending on your country's healthcare system, offer a route to accessible and inclusive dance provision. As the following case study will explore, social prescribing involves many stakeholders and can have significant impact for a range of participants.

DANCE THROUGH YOUR DOCTOR: DANCE ON PRESCRIPTION

Dance Network Association, UK

The Dance Network Association, otherwise known as DNA, is one of a number of organisations in the UK that offer dance as a social prescription activity. DNA's work promotes community happiness through creative dancing and has two strands to the practice. The first, 'Dancing for Joy', provides inclusive sessions for older adults, individuals with conditions like dementia and Parkinson's, and for mothers at risk of postnatal depression, along with their infants and young children. The second strand, Dance for Education, involves big Mass Dance projects, bespoke school curriculum and after school projects and intergenerational work where the organisation links schools with care settings. These programmes aim to advance dance education but also have health benefits, for example, activities aimed at lowering obesity rates.

The organisation has worked (and continues to work) to build a network of providers in the hope that they will become DNA Hosts. As a 'DNA Host' GP's and link workers advise members/patients about DNA's activity by providing them with their contact details and information about the programme. Those who are referred are enrolled on a class programme and can access free dance activity. The team also works with the Alzheimer's Society and Parkinson's UK and prescribes to members that they work with. Guided by these collaborations, DNA addresses needs identified by different communities and organisations and translates them into tangible outcomes (Fig. 12).

Reducing social isolation is one of the core drivers of DNA's work, as well as being proactive in the prevention of social isolation, the impactful symptoms of neurological conditions and post-natal depression. The work, according to G. Wright (personal communication, 2024), alters or complements a medical approach seeking to address health conditions/concerns, supporting people to prevent, eradicate and manage their symptoms through dancing. The COVID-19 pandemic exacerbated experiences of loneliness and isolation, particularly for older adults who lived alone. During this period, DNA provided access to classes online, which it continues to do, and it also has a video library of classes available on their website that people can access. This acknowledges the need for some people to be introduced to the practice ahead of joining classes; it can be a big step. This video library also offers

Source: Photo credit: Rachel Cherry.

Fig. 12. DNA Dancing with Dementia Class.

the practice to those who might not be able to physically access the classes in-person.

> *The dance classes run for an hour and a half in all of the programmes, no matter what it is, and it's really vital for us to have an hour of creative activity. It is also essential to have half an hour of social time, which we've done for our whole history, and that sometimes is more important for the peer support network, the bonding, the relationships that are created, the friendships that are made. This is the time for people to vent and feel like they're connected to other people that are going through the same difficulties. (G. Wright, personal communication, CEO and Founder, DNA, 2024)*

The dance activity in the sessions is mainly seated, although there are options offered to all to stand, but G. Wright (personal communication, 2024) is very keen that the practice is not labelled as exercise. Some may refer to the session content as exercise, but the team wants to emphasise its identity as dance and creative practice. The session leaders utilise props and music as important stimuli for movement and also as collective tools for interaction with one another.

According to the organisation, workshop leaders have observed a reduction in loneliness for the participants, but they also recognise the cognitive benefits of learning something new, particular for those with dementia or Parkinson's (G. Wright, personal communication, 2024). The processes of focusing on a new activity and engaging in creative movement are beneficial in terms of the memory recall.

DNA provides support to isolated adults, mums at risk of postnatal depression and those with specific conditions, alongside their caregivers, and emphasises the importance of social interaction and fostering friendships during classes which offer an opportunity to move with those who have similar life experiences.

As this case study has highlighted, having local, community-based access to dance is important for raising participation levels and for offering dance to as many people as possible. Another route for this is through school provision and continuing creative and physical education. Advocating for dance in education as another way of addressing public health concerns through dance is important, especially as the dominant forms of physical education in schools, such as team sports, are not favoured by all students. Dance can offer an alternative to competitive or team activities and still address the health and wellbeing concerns of children and young people, including rising obesity rates, growing mental health issues and the implications of greater social media and technology use (see the DAZL case study in Chapter 3 for more on this).

As part of offering dance sessions and addressing access in relation to this, studios, classes and performances should be accessible to all people. In some cases, this means taking dance to people, such as the examples in the case studies of Chapters 2 and 5 where dance activity is provided within acute health environments. In other cases, this means attending to the access needs of participants by ensuring that venues are physically accessible and that class content can be understood by all and offers different levels at which to access the material. Access to dance sessions might also mean breaking down attitudinal barriers to dance, particularly perceptions of who 'can' and 'cannot' dance or of what dance is, which can be addressed through greater visibility and representation of different bodies in dance.

OVERCOMING GLOBAL AND FUTURE CHALLENGES

In recent years, the world has witnessed significant changes and unprecedented challenges brought about by worldwide pandemics, wars and political shifts. These challenges are exacerbated and caused by the effects of climate change, rising inactivity levels, long-term impacts of the COVID-19 pandemic and the growing mental health crisis. Person-centred approaches pioneered by dance practitioners, and increasingly by healthcare workers, are vital to overcome challenges faced by the general public, societies and the wider world. Collaboration will also be key in order to alleviate pressure on certain systems and to innovate in order to evolve.

The rise in the online provision of dance classes and workshops, largely as a result of the COVID-19 pandemic, has enabled people who might not have been able to access in-person dance classes to engage with dance (Kolb & Haitzinger, 2023). While these may have an negative impact on income streams for dance artists, they can be impactful in positive ways. As many of our case studies have documented, online interaction and other practices brought about during the height of the COVID-19 pandemic have continued, to recognise that not everyone has stopped shielding from the pandemic. In times of crisis, we are often forced to find new ways to do things that can offer a new way of seeing things.

In the past few years, we have seen a great rise in financial crises across the world, with the impact of conflicts, COVID-19 and political unrest leading to a cost-of-living crisis. These financial pressures not only affect individuals and their disposable income but also impact how organisations and healthcare sectors must manage their budgets. This squeezing of finances has an impact on decisions made by healthcare providers. Often the arts, due to being viewed as a 'luxury', are one of the first things to be cut from budgets; however, they might also be the solution to tackling one of the biggest issues emerging from this crisis that of the mass decline in mental health. Statistics of those facing financial hardship demonstrate a clear correlation between struggling financially and declining mental health (ONS, 2022). Yet, as evidence in this book shows, dance can significantly alleviate the symptoms of poor mental health through social connection, connecting with the body and creative expression, thus indicating that the arts, in general, and dance, in particular, can have a long-term importance of the arts in tackling some of the effects of the cost-of-living crisis, rather than being viewed simply as a frivolous luxury.

The rise in technological innovation, particularly the rise of artificial intelligence (AI), has led to great debate regarding its potentially negative impact on humans, society and our autonomy as humans. For some, it raises concerns over the weaponisation of technology and its displacement of human activity, while others see the potential of technology to revolutionise how beneficial activities such as health care are organised, managed and respond to the needs of the population. Whatever your view, there will be continued developments in digital technology and, as dance artist Lucinda Jarrett (2024) highlights, they 'will become more important [in healthcare practice] as we seek to create aesthetic frames that will enable the patient voice to project itself in an increasingly undiluted medium'. Detailed in the following case study is how the use of virtual reality (VR) is enhancing and better communicating patient lived experience of health and health care through engagement with dance and performance.

OPENING NEW MOVEMENT CAPACITIES WITH CREATIVE TECHNOLOGIES

CoDa Dance Company, UK

In the UK, 1 in 6 people live with at least one neurological condition, which equates to 16.5 million people (The Neurological Alliance, 2022). Neurological conditions, including multiple sclerosis (MS), Parkinson's and acquired brain injuries commonly lead to limited mobility, reduced cognitive functioning and memory impairment, often requiring care support for day-to-day living. Artistic Director, Nikki Watson, was motivated to begin CoDa Dance Company in 2013 after experience within her own family when she discovered a lack of movement classes for those with MS. She set up CoDa to fill this gap and challenge the stereotypes and expectations of those with neurological conditions.

Since 2017, CoDa Dance Company has been working with the Royal Hospital for Neuro-disability in London to deliver weekly dance sessions across nine wards, which have been shown to offer participants statistically significant increases in energy levels (Fig. 13). They have also been developing performance work that integrates creative technologies to share the hidden stories of people living with neurological conditions.

The creative technology CoDa uses includes VR, augmented reality, motion capture, depth cameras, green screens, projection mapping and wearable tech. The tech they currently use most is a depth camera – a Kinect Azure device which reads the body(ies) in space, turns that/those body shape/s into data, which their Creative Technologists convert into a beautifully designed visual image which is shown on a huge screen. As the dancers move in the space,

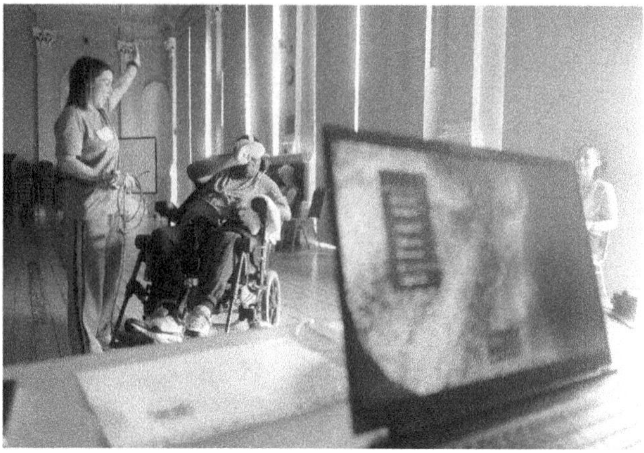

Source: Image credit: Cave and Sky. Photo credit: CoDa Dance Company.

Fig. 13. Neurodisabled Lived Experience Consultant Using the Interactive Experience He'd Co-created with CoDa Dance.

they can see the designed visuals change in response to their movements on screen, in a way making their bodies game controllers of a large scale digital art work. The way the visuals interact with the dancer's movements is designed to inspire the dancer to explore and experiment with the potential of what they can make the digital artwork do.

Using VR, CoDa have also converted this interactive experience further by use of a headset that shows the individual wearing it the visuals within a virtual, different space to the one they are physically in. This approach can offer a sense of depersonalisation, a form of out-of-body experience that has been linked to pain reduction and euphoria, which is evidenced through anecdotes the company has collected:

> *It's like I'm floating. I have no pain. It's like I'm having an out of body experience and my Parkinson's is gone. (VR participant)*

> *The perspective is third person, mirroring yourself, out of body experience as opposed to being first person. Gives it a reflective, personal experience. Visuals are very nice. Feels evocative of different sensory experiences. (VR audience member)*

The company emphasises the importance and value of collective group experiences, with the social benefit of connecting with others who experience similar conditions and moving together. When interacting with the technologies as a group, they have a common experience, and they can create visual reactions together, which can amplify group interaction. This leads not only to a physically invigorating experience but also to a social one, with both the physical and digital space encouraging negotiation, exploration and synergy.

> *We've seen in community [settings] that using creative technology, for example in a seated session, we get into the interaction and straight away people are up and out of their seats, moving bigger than they had been previously in the session when they had been seated. People are moving in novel, new ways because there's an extra feedback loop visually. When they're controlling the reactive imagery on the screen, they [realise] 'oh, what can I make it do?'. This is dance activity that unlocks new movement capacities in people, and if you're physically unlocking new movement there's potentially new neural pathways being activated or old ones being reactivated, which has huge implications for rehabilitation of neurological conditions. (E. Phillips, personal communication, Executive Director and Creative Producer, 2024)*

Co-creative methods are at the heart of CoDa's practice because lived experience is a central tenet of the values that underpin the company. Feedback from audiences and participants influences changes that are made to the technologies, from designing how the interactions behave through to colour choices. This has led the company to employ a group of neurodisabled lived experience consultants who collaborate with the artistic director throughout the creation process, from ideation of concept to shaping content to technological design. This helps shape how the experiences are communicated to audiences, aiming to reflect authentically something of the experiences people with neurological conditions or neurodisabilities have.

> *The way that we make work has been part of our practice for a long, long time and people didn't always get our*

> *work. They were like: is it participation or is it performance? And it's both – one informs the other. Now people understand that more and co-creation is popular now. And how co-creation is done varies amongst companies and what makes it super important is that it gives people a voice. It raises the standard of art that is being produced, and it remains true and real and raw, giving people a platform to be able to open up conversation. It levels the playing field for everybody who's in the room together. They have a shared experience. (N. Watson, personal communication, Artistic Director, 2024)*

This is important for people sharing the experience as well, who say:

> *Seeing my symptoms brought to life through light & dance was fascinating. I've never been able to fully explain it, but I really felt the dancers showed what it feels like for me each day. (Lived Experience Consultant)*

> *Seeing her not being able to stand up, that's me getting up out of bed every day. I don't talk about it but that's my truth. (Lived Experience Consultant)*

The importance of embedding lived experience into the design of CoDa's work is not only impactful for the participants but also in communicating this experience to family members, carers and clinical staff. The use of technology and bodily movement can translate experiences that are difficult to articulate or communicate verbally to those who don't have personal lived experience of it.

> *It's important for participants to see themselves reflected in the cultural sphere. We know that representation is hugely important and neurological conditions aren't typically in the public sphere and if they are, they're really, really rare. So for people to be like 'that's me, that's my experience' is really huge. Equally for family members, clinicians and specialist staff to be able to say 'ohh I get it, this is what they've been talking about. This is the symptom they've been trying to explain to me and I haven't*

> *understood. And now I understand it'. That's what the work is for – to raise awareness – so that neuro disabled people can see themselves reflected back in the cultural sphere, and to have that validation that they're part of society, that they're valuable enough to be represented in that way. (Philips, 2024)*

HOW MIGHT THE BARRIERS BE DIFFERENT FOR PROFESSIONALS?

Many of the aspects and issues discussed in this chapter speak to the experience for professionals as well as participants. Challenges such as access, dealing with global crises and dealing with self-doubt are shared experiences. However, both healthcare and dance practitioners need to look after themselves, 'as the saying goes, you cannot pour from an empty cup, and just as artists/practitioners feed their practice with fresh ideas and inspiration, their own health and wellbeing also requires nourishment' (Collard-Stokes & Yoon Irons, 2022, p. 62). Barriers and challenges can make self-care for practitioners more difficult, so this section will briefly explore practitioner-specific challenges and present some ways to mitigate them and some opportunities for further developing their practice (in addition to the ideas explored in Chapter 5).

Barriers to dance for healthcare professionals are also related to their personal experience of dancing, so discussions regarding self-doubt, perception of dance and confidence may influence to what extent they embrace dance. Similarly, one of the greatest battles for a dance artist is in breaking down attitudinal barriers about what dance is and what it can provide for people's health and wellbeing. There is more work to be done to demonstrate and evidence the full and nuanced impact of dance for health and wellbeing, and more investment in research is one way to address this. Advocacy and representation of dance in all its forms can also help combat misconceptions or lack of understanding about dance.

One of the key takeaways from our discussions with dance practitioners who work in health and care settings is the importance of the work that goes into making the relationships and partnerships strong. This should not be underestimated and involves buy in from all. Often it takes someone in a position of power to invest in the practice of dance within healthcare settings, and so dance (and the arts more generally) is subject to gatekeeping within health. As indicated in the previous chapter, trained dance artists are equipped with the knowledge, skills and experience of managing a dance space and supporting those within it. This is one of the key reasons why we encourage healthcare workers to work in collaboration with dance artists to deliver dance activity.

Part of the collaboration between health and dance is tackling the differences in language and values. As indicated in many of our case studies, health and dance can have differing approaches to touch, power dynamics and spatial use. In addition, terminology can be used in different ways, which can lead to misunderstandings or tensions. This is often why the development of fruitful working relationships takes time, but the benefits and the strength gained by taking that time to understand one another as practitioners and everyone's role in facilitating the practice, is worthwhile. Thinking about how dancers communicate about their practice and evidence the impact is also key to building the practice and helping to better inform healthcare workers, such as GPs, about the opportunities for health that dance provides.

An approach to dance for health practice that has inclusive principles at its core can benefit all. For dance practitioners, this can involve sharing access information for venues and classes very publicly, asking participants if they have any access needs (and accommodating these) or adapting session content so that it uses non-ableist language and open instructions. One Dance UK (2023) developed the *Considering Difference* resource, in collaboration with a range of dance artists and researchers, which provides questions, prompts and advice for practitioners on how to ensure their provision is accessible. In addition, there are many continuing professional development (CPD) opportunities for dance artists, and for healthcare professionals, with many being offered free of charge. For more information on CPD opportunities worldwide, see the resource links in the next chapter.

CONCLUDING THOUGHTS

Dance is a wonderful source of joy, bodily engagement and social connection. As we have seen in this final chapter, dance also comes with its challenges. We have sought to investigate some of the barriers or tensions that are present in the design, negotiation and delivery of dancing for health initiatives, for both the participating individual and for practitioners. In this way, we have been able to consider ways to mitigate risks, overcome personal biases and tackle access barriers to dance.

Through this book, we hope that many of you will feel empowered, inspired and confident in pursuing dancing for health or advocating for your own dancing for health journey. To conclude, we wanted to offer three ways of navigating that journey.

Participate in *Dancing*

We have strived to demonstrate that dance is for everyone irrespective of age, fitness level, disability or location. Wherever you are located in the world, you should find local, community-based access to dance. You can start with this book's resource section, coming up in the next section, although a simple internet search for your area should offer a range of additional options. You might want to try out several styles. Remember that the best way to discover if we like something is to ask ourselves if we would like to do it again. If you don't, then perhaps try a new style. If you do, then you have found your best medicine!

Experience *Dancing*

Seeing and experiencing more dance can expand your understanding of what dance can be and who can participate! Dance is often shown on television, in movies and is available online to observe. There is nothing quite like live performance and across the world there are dance performances of all genres and styles, and in many different settings, including at outdoor festivals, in regional theatres and in museums and cultural venues. What dance will you go to see next?

Advocate for *Dancing*

Dancing for health and wellbeing is a relatively new concept and area of practice, one that is growing. A wealth of studies have already evidenced dance's positive impact on people and society, yet further research is needed to continue to reveal more of its healing qualities. As a health professional or a dancer you can engage in advocating for the development of more programmes, schemes and courses dedicated to enhancing the contribution of dance to health and wellbeing.

7

USEFUL LINKS AND RESOURCES

Here are a selection of resources that promote or encourage engagement and involvement in dance. Use these to learn more about particular practices of dance organisations.

RESOURCES USED IN THE BOOK

Akademi, UK – https://www.akademi.co.uk/

CoDa Dance Company, UK – https://codadance.com/

Dança e Parkinson, Brazil – https://www.instagram.com/dancaeparkinson/

Dance Action Zone Leeds (DAZL), UK – http://dazl.org.uk/

Dance Health Alliance, Australia – https://www.dancehealthalliance.org.au/

Dance Move Feel, UK – https://www.movedancefeel.com/

Dance Network Association, UK – https://www.dancenetworkassociation.org.uk/

DanceSyndrome, UK – https://dancesyndrome.co.uk/

Fillipa Pereira-Stubbs, UK – http://www.fpereirastubbs.co.uk/dance/dance-for-health/

Move Dance Feel, UK – https://www.movedancefeel.com/

Moving Tu Balance, UK – https://www.instagram.com/movingtubalance/

Small Things Dance Collective, UK – https://www.smallthingsdance.co.uk/

Steady and Strong Dance, UK – https://www.hants.gov.uk/socialcareandhealth/adultsocialcare/falls-prevention/danceclasses

Stories in the Moment, USA – https://magdakaczmarska.com/

Stuart Pimsler Dance Theatre Company, USA – http://www.stuartpimsler.com/arts-healthcare

ZoieLogic Dance Theatre, UK – https://zoielogic.co.uk/

FURTHER LINKS

American Dance Therapy Association, USA – https://adta.memberclicks.net/

Arts and Health, Ireland – https://www.artsandhealth.ie/

Dance Movement Therapy Association in Canada, Canada – https://www.dmtac.org/

Dance Movement Therapy Association of Australasia, Australia – https://dtaa.org.au/

Dance to Health from Aesop, UK – https://dancetohealth.org/

Dancemind, UK – https://dancemind.co.uk/

Dance Network Association, UK – https://www.dancenetworkassociation.org.uk/videolibrary

English National Ballet, UK – https://www.ballet.org.uk/get-involved/dance-health/

Jabadao, UK – https://www.jabadao.org/developmental-movement-play-approach

International Association for Dance Medicine and Science, Worldwide – https://iadms.org/

Mature Artists Dance Experience (MADE), Australia – https://madecompany.com.au/about/

Mark Morris Dance Group, USA – https://markmorrisdancegroup.org/community/pd/dance-for-pd/

One Dance UK, UK – https://www.onedanceuk.org/

People Dancing, UK – https://www.communitydance.org.uk/

Popping for Parkinson, UK – https://www.poppingforparkinsons.com

Rosetta Life, UK – https://rosettalife.org/

Scottish Ballet, UK – https://scottishballet.co.uk/move-with-us/dance-health/

Step Up for Parkinson's, Malta – https://stepupforparkinsons.com/

The Association for Dance Movement Psychotherapy, UK – https://admp.org.uk/

The Somatic Practice and Chronic Pain Network, UK and International – https://somaticandpain.coventry.domains/

Examples of Dance Activities in Care Homes

Dancesing Care – https://dancesingcare.uk

InMature Company, Leeds – https://yorkshiredance.com/project/in-mature-company

Creative Encounters, Spitalfields Music – https://spitalfieldsmusic.org.uk/events/creative-encounters

Hip Hop in Care Home – https://www.theblairacademy.com

Online Classes

Flamingo Chicks inclusive virtual classes for children – https://flamingochicks.org/athome

Dance for Kids classes from Stop Gap Dance Company – https://www.stopgapdance.com/learn-and-practice/youth-and-community/youth/dance-for-kids-with-iris

Home Practice Stop Gap Dance Company – http://bit.ly/StopgapHomePractice

Pineapple Dance Studios online classes – https://www.pineapple.uk.com/pages/pineapple-live

Contemplative Dance Practice – https://myriadicity.net/contact-improvisation/online-movement-collaboration/an-online-contemplative-movement-score

News Articles

6 reasons to dance yourself back to health, British Heart Foundation – https://www.bhf.org.uk/informationsupport/heart-matters-magazine/activity/6-reasons-to-dance-your-way-to-health

Dance Like Your Doctor Is Watching: It's Great for Your Mind and Body, Time Magazine, 20 December 2018 – https://time.com/5484237/dancing-health-benefits/

Dancing fitness: why you're never too old to dance and reap all of the benefits, Stylist Magazine – https://www.stylist.co.uk/fitness-health/wellbeing/dancing-fitness-never-too-old-dance-benefits-2/571571

Get to twerk: why dancing is a wellbeing superpower, Financial Times, 6 April 2021 – https://www.ft.com/content/04fab451-e7fa-41df-873c-2e9b0ba58445

Healthy Reasons To Get Dancing Around Your Living Room Today, 28 July 2019 – https://www.forbes.com/sites/daniellebrooker/2019/07/28/healthy-reasons-to-get-dancing-around-your-living-room-today/?sh=3ffbaa4f673d

Podcasts

Meditation – https://open.spotify.com/episode/7n2U5lU0ts0gAcP9q4gd1K?si=a1e445ca8d594a99

Why dancing is the best way to enhance your brain and fitness – https://www.bbc.co.uk/programmes/articles/1Hpr6R1f4M7f8Qc6fPGH2hg/why-dancing-is-the-best-way-to-enhance-your-brain-and-fitness

The Power of Dance – join Dame Darcey Bussell and Dr Peter Lovatt as they discuss the many health benefits of dance for health – https://open.spotify.com/episode/7HhHgiWPWhruD6zJWYdJhV

Music and Movement for Health and Wellbeing of Older Adults – https://www.podomatic.com/podcasts/universitylimerick/episodes/2023-09-22T04_43_36-07_00

Is dance movement therapy an effective intervention for dementia? A review of the evidence – https://podcasts.apple.com/us/podcast/is-dance-movement-therapy-an-effective-intervention/id276923202?i=1000637923486

Toolkits and Scores

The Small Dance Score – https://myriadicity.net/contact-improv/learning-contact-improvisation/steve-paxtons-1977-small-dance-guidance

Dance on Toolkit has been written for dancers, care home staff, public health professionals, health and social care practitioners – https://getdoncastermoving.org/dance-on-toolkit

Active Ingredients: The Aesop planning and evaluation model for Arts with a Social Purpose – https://ae-sop.org/wp-content/uploads/sites/63/2018/09/Active-Ingredients-Report-Sept-2018-Final-low-res.pdf

Toolkit for Care Staff

Bringing dance into care settings for older people – https://www.pdsw.org.uk/wp-content/uploads/2018/04/Breathe-Arts-for-Health-Cornwall-Dance-Toolkit-for-Care-Homes.pdf

Music Playlists

Dancing with Young People – https://open.spotify.com/playlist/6rfPY4D3KDbKWdNa51uvFG

Creative Dancing – https://open.spotify.com/playlist/7K8j9a4h6qwRDz7KKuFVe0

Dancing with Older People – https://open.spotify.com/playlist/1erCdBobIKeQcoWF7Tx9JN

ABOUT THE AUTHORS

Noyale Colin (MA/PhD) is currently the interim course leader for the MA in Expanded Practice at the London Contemporary Dance School (LCDS). Previously, she was a senior lecturer at the University of Winchester (UoW), UK, where she taught theory and practice across all levels of the undergraduate BA Dance and Performing Arts, including contemporary dance and somatic practices.

She studied at the Conservatoires of Nantes and Lyon, before training in postmodern dance and presenting work at leading performing spaces in New York City. She subsequently pursued her career by exploring different movement and somatic practices including yoga, shiatsu and improvisation. She led the Dance department at the University of Suffolk, UK, from 2012 to 2015.

She is a Senior Fellow of the Higher Education Academy. In 2018, she assumed the role of Convenor of the University's *Centre for Performance Practice and Research (CPPR)*. In 2020, she was appointed Leader of the *REF UoA for the Performing Arts department*.

She is Co-editor of two books, *Collaboration in Performance Practices: Premises, Workings and Failures* (Palgrave Macmillan, 2016) and *Ethical Agility in Dance: Rethinking Technique in British Contemporary Dance* (Routledge, 2023); she writes journal articles and produces practical works related to her research around issues of embodied practices and the notion of the collaborative self in performance. She is Co-editor of a special edition of *Performance Research Journal on Solidarity* (2023). Current projects include a research network project around the expanded field of dance in health, focusing on activities around fall prevention. She is a Qualified Biodynamic Craniosacral Therapist (2024).

She has extensive experience organising public engagement events such as book launches, talks and podcasts. She also ran community projects engaging university students with general public and health practitioners through intergenerational dance projects, inclusive dance workshops, roundtables on neurodiversity in HE and spirituality in dance. She is a Member of the institute of contemplative practices at UoW and one of the executive board members (secretary) of *Dance HE.*

Kathryn Stamp (PGCE/MA/PhD) is a Dance Researcher and Educator, specialising in inclusive dance practice and the value of dance and dance in education. Working as Assistant Professor at the Centre for Dance Research (C-DaRE) at Coventry University, she has explored the lived experience of remote working for disabled dance artists, and the impact of the COVID-19 pandemic. In 2020, she completed her PhD at C-DaRE and her AHRC-funded research focused on public interventions that sought to change perceptions about disabled people who dance. Recently, she has worked on the *'Strictly' Inclusive* project funded by the AHRC and the BBC and co-leads the AHRC-funded Critical Dance Pedagogy network in collaboration with Canterbury Christ Church University.

She graduated with an MA in Education (Distinction) from the University of Brighton, UK, (2016) and holds a first-class BA (Hons) in Dance Studies from Roehampton University, UK, (2010). Her Masters dissertation focused on the perceptions held by dance students as to the value of dance and its effect on aspects of life, including education, relationships and wellbeing. She has long been involved in dance education, having completed her PGCE (Dance) at the University of Brighton and having taught across secondary schools and FE colleges in the South of England. She has worked as an Academic Tutor at Bird College, Research Assistant at the University of Winchester, UK, and Associate Lecturer at the University of Malta, Malta, the University of Lincoln, UK and the University of Wolverhampton, UK.

In 2024 she published *Ethical Agility in Dance: Rethinking Technique in British Contemporary Dance* (co-edited with Noyale

Colin and Cathy Seago) a book on dance technique (Routledge). She is Chair of the *Society for Dance Research*, a Board Member for *Dance HE*, and former Editorial Manager for the *Journal of Dance and Somatic Practices*. She worked with the Sport and Recreation Alliance to develop a report around the Social Benefit of Dance and Movement (2023). She is an Ambassador for *AWA DANCE charity* and an Advisory Board member for *We Are Epic*.

REFERENCES

Adair, C. (1992). Cultured bodies – The social construction of the body. In Women and Dance (Ed.), *Women in society series list* (edCG). Palgrave. https://doi.org/10.1007/978-1-349-22374-9_3

ADMP UK. (2023). *The association for dance movement psychotherapy*. https://admp.org.uk/

Aesop. (2020). *Dance to health: Phase 1 roll-out 'test and learn' evaluation report*. https://ae-sop.org/wp-content/uploads/sites/63/2020/06/AESOP-Dance-to-Health-Phase-1-Overall-evaluation-Report-April-2020-FINAL.pdf

AfHW APPG. (2017). *Creative health: The arts for health and wellbeing*. The short report. https://www.culturehealthandwellbeing.org.uk/appg-inquiry/Publications/Creative_Health_The_Short_Report.pdf

Akādemi. (2017). *Dance well resource book*. Akādemi. https://www.akademi.co.uk/wp-content/uploads/2017/10/DANCE-WELL-BOOK-2017_web.pdf

Akandere, M., & Demir, B. (2011). The effect of dance over depression. *Collegium Antropologicum*, *35*(3), 651–656. https://pubmed.ncbi.nlm.nih.gov/22053537/

Archbold, V., & Bond, S. (2020). *Dance Action Zone Leeds (DAZL): Mental health and resilience project 2019/2020 Public Health Leeds funded evaluation report*. https://eprints.leedsbeckett.ac.uk/id/eprint/7485/10/DanceActionZoneLeedsPV-ARCHBOLD.pdf

Arts for Health Cornwall and Isles of Scilly (AFHC). (2010). *Dancing for older peoples' health and well-being toolkit*. https://www.pdsw.org.uk/wp-content/uploads/2018/04/Breathe-Arts-for-Health-Cornwall-Dance-Toolkit-for-Care-Homes.pdf

Basso, J. C., Satyal, M. K., & Rugh, R. (2021). Dance on the brain: Enhancing intra- and inter-brain synchrony. *Frontiers in Human Neuroscience*, *14*(584312), 1–23. https://10.3389/fnhum.2020.584312

Benjamin, A. (2010). CABBAGES AND KINGS: Disability, dance and some timely considerations. In A. Carter & J. O'Shea (Eds.), *Routledge dance studies reader* (pp. 111–121). Routledge.

Beute, F., & de Kort, Y. A. W. (2014). Natural resistance: Exposure to nature and self-regulation, mood, and physiology after ego-depletion. *Journal of Environmental Psychology*, *40*(December), 167–178. https://doi.org/10.1016/j.jenvp.2014.06.004

Blackwell, S., & Blackwell, J. (2023). *'If it needs doing…' Reflections on a decade of DanceSyndrome* (Animated ed., pp. 36–39). People Dancing.

Blades, H. (2018). Dance's political imaginaries. In S. Ellis, H. Blades, & C. Waelde (Eds.), *A world of muscle and bone* (pp. 87–111). C-DaRE.

Blanco-Rambo, E., Bandeira-Guimarães, M., Vieira, A. F., PiettaDias, C., Izquierdo, M., & Cadore, E. L. (2022). Dance as an intervention to reduce fall risk in older adults: A systematic review with a meta-analysis. *The Journal of Aging and Physical Activity*, *30*(6), 1118–1132. https://pubmed.ncbi.nlm.nih.gov/35500909/

Breathe Arts Health. (2020, November 11). *Breathe wellbeing workshops: Indian dance for mind and body with Rachel Waterman* [Video]. YouTube. https://www.youtube.com/watch?v=95mTzXd5fJs

Brendtro, L. (2017). Touch: The foundation of belonging. *CF Learning*, *1*(8), 1–9. https://growingedgetraining.com/wp-content/uploads/2017/10/Touch-Foundation-of-Belonging_Thriving_vol_1-8.pdf

British Heart Foundation [BHF]. (n.d.). 6 reasons to dance your way back to health. *Heart Matters*. https://www.bhf.org.uk/informationsupport/heart-matters-magazine/activity/6-reasons-to-dance-your-way-to-health

Broderick, S. (2011). Arts practices in unreasonable doubt? Reflections on understandings of arts practices in healthcare contexts. *Arts & Health*, *3*(2), 95–109. https://doi.org/10.1080/17533015.2010.551716

Burkhardt, J., & Brennan, C. (2012). The effects of recreational dance interventions on the health and well-being of children and young people: A systematic review. *Arts & Health: An International Journal for Research, Policy and Practice*, *4*(2), 148–161. https://doi.org/10.1080/17533015.2012.665810

Byrka, K., & Ryczko, N. (2018). Positive effects of dancing in natural versus indoor settings: The mediating role of engagement in physical activity. *Journal of Environmental Psychology*, *57*(June), 25–33. https://doi.org/10.1016/j.jenvp.2018.06.002

Catterall, J. S., & Peppler, K. A. (2007). Learning in the visual arts and the worldviews of young children. *Cambridge Journal of Education*, *37*(4), 543–560.

Cervi, L. (2021). Tik Tok and generation Z, theatre. *Dance and Performance Training*, *12*(2), 198–204. https://doi.org/10.1080/19443927.2021.1915617

Chappell, K., Redding, E., Crickmay, U., Stancliffe, R., Jobbins, V., & Smith, S. (2021). The aesthetic, artistic and creative contributions of dance for health and wellbeing across the lifecourse: A systematic review. *International Journal of Qualitative Studies on Health and Well-being*, *16*(1), 1–20. https://doi.org/10.1080/17482631.2021.1950891

Cherriere, C., Martel, M., Sarrasin, A., Ballaz, L., Tallet, J., & Lemay, M. (2020). Benefits of a dance intervention on balance in adolescents with cerebral palsy. *Physical & Occupational Therapy in Pediatrics*, *40*(5), 518–533. https://doi.org/10.1080/01942638.2020.1720053

Christensen, J. F., & Chang, D. S. (2021). *Dancing is the best medicine: The science of how moving to a beat is good for body, brain, and soul.* Greystone Books Ltd.

Clift, S., Phillips, K., & Pritchard, S. (2021). The need for robust critique of research on social and health impacts of the arts. *Cultural Trends*, *30*(5), 442–459. https://doi.org/10.1080/09548963.2021.1910492

Collard-Stokes, G., & Yoon Irons, J. (2022). Artist wellbeing: Exploring the experiences of dance artists delivering community health and wellbeing initiatives. *Research in Dance Education*, *23*(1), 60–74. https://doi.org/10.1080/14647893.2021.1993176

Collinson, P. (2020). When the body makes its presence felt: Somatic-informed movement practice as an integral part of the hospital care team.

Journal of Dance & Somatic Practices, *12*(2), 289–302. https://doi.org/10.1386/jdsp_00029_1

Cooper Albright, A. (1997). *Choreographing difference: The body and identity in contemporary dance*. Wesleyan University Press.

Cruz-Ferreira, A., Marmeleira, J., Formigo, A., Gomes, D., & Fernandes, J. (2015). Creative dance improves physical fitness and life satisfaction in older women. *Research on Aging*, *37*(8), 837–855. https://doi.org/10.1177/0164027514568103

Cummings, J. (2017). We should all support #EndPJparalysis. *NHS*. https://www.england.nhs.uk/blog/jane-cummings-32/

Dadswell, A., Bungay, H., Wilson, C., & Munn-Giddings, C. (2020). The impact of participatory arts in promoting social relationships for older people within care homes. *Perspectives in Public Health*, *140*(5), 286–293. https://doi.org/10.1177/1757913920921204

DanceSyndrome. (2022, August 2). *DanceSyndrome launches ground-breaking NHS video project*. DanceSyndrome. https://dancesyndrome.co.uk/nhs-video-project/

DanceSyndrome. (2024). *What we do*. DanceSyndrome. https://dancesyndrome.co.uk/what-we-do/

Darivemula, S., Bhatia, R., & Bhumi, S. (2021). Dancing doctors: Exploring the potential of cultural dance education to improve cultural competency and clinical communication. *Public Health*, *195*, 22–23. https://doi.org/10.1016/j.puhe.2021.03.019

Delabary, M. D. S., Loch Sbeghen, I., Wolffenbuttel, M., Pereira, D. R., & Haas, A. N. (2022). Online dance classes during the Covid-19 pandemic: New challenges and teaching strategies for the 'Dance & Parkinson's at home' project. *Research in Dance Education*, *25*(1), 1–19. https://doi.org/10.1080/14647893.2022.2083595

Dennen, V. P., Choi, H., & Word, K. (2020). Social media, teenagers, and the school context: A scoping review of research in education and related fields. *Education Technology Research and Development*, *68*, 1635–1658. https://doi.org/10.1007/s11423-020-09796-z

Dowler, L. (2016). Can improvised somatic dance reduce acute pain for young people in hospital?. *Nursing Children and Young People*, *28*(9), 20–25. https://doi.org/10.7748/ncyp.2016.e740

Duberg, A., Möller, M., & Sunvisson, H. (2016). "I feel free": Experiences of a dance intervention for adolescent girls with internalizing problems. *International Journal of Qualitative Studies on Health and Well-Being*, *11*(1), 31946. https://doi.org/10.3402/qhw.v11.31946

Dwarika, M. S., & Haraldsen, H. M. (2023). Mental health in dance: A scoping review. *Frontiers in Psychology*, *14*, 1090645. https://doi.org/10.3389/fpsyg.2023.1090645

Elliott, M., & Gardner, P. (2018). The role of music in the lives of older adults with dementia ageing in place: A scoping review. *Dementia*, *17*(2), 199–213. https://doi.org/10.1177/1471301216639424

Fancourt, D., Perkins, R., Ascenso, S., Carvalho, L., Steptoe, A., & Williamon, A. (2016). Effects of group drumming interventions on anxiety, depression, social resilience and inflammatory immune response among mental health service users. *PLoS One*, *11*(3), 1–16. https://doi.org/10.1371%2Fjournal.pone.0151136

Fitzpatrick, D., Doyle, K., Finn, G., & Gallagher, P. (2019). Pyjama paralysis: Time to make a move!. *Age and Ageing*, *48*(3), 1–6. https://doi.org/10.1093/ageing/afz102.54

Fong Yan, A., Cobley, S., Chan, C., Pappas, E., Nicholson, L. L., Ward, R. E., Murdoch, R. E., Gu, Y., Trevor, B. L., Vassallo, A. J., Wewege, M. A., & Hiller, C. E. (2018). The effectiveness of dance interventions on physical health outcomes compared to other forms of physical activity: A systematic review and meta-analysis. *Sports Medicine*, *48*, 933–951. https://doi.org/10.1007/s40279-017-0853-5

Froggett, L., & Little, R. (2012). Dance as a complex intervention in an acute mental health setting: A place 'in-between'. *British Journal of Occupational Therapy*, *75*(2), 93–99.

Garnett, A., Hui, L., Oleynikov, C., & Boamah, S. (2023). Compassion fatigue in healthcare providers: A scoping review. *BMC Health Services Research*, *23*(1336), 1–16. https://doi.org/10.1186/s12913-023-10356-3

Goldberg, D. S., & Mcgee, S. J. (2011). Pain as a global public health priority. *BMC Public Health*, *11*(770), 1–5. https://doi.org/10.1186%2F1471-2458-11-770

Golding, S. (2023). *Moving tu balance*. https://www.movingtubalance.co.uk/about

Gomaa, Y., Slade, S., Tamplin, J., Wittwer, J., Gray, R., Blackberry, I., & Morris, M. (2020). Therapeutic dancing for frail older people in residential aged care: A thematic analysis of barriers and facilitators to implementation. *The International Journal of Aging and Human Development*, *90*(4), 403–422. https://doi.org/10.1177/0091415019854775

Grau, A. (1998). *Dance*. Dorling Kindersley.

Green Candle Dance. (2016). *Evaluating the impact of dance activities for people in different stages of dementia*. https://www.greencandledance.com/about/reports

Guzmán-García, A., Hughes, J. C., James, I. A., & Rochester, L. (2013). Dancing as a psychosocial intervention in care homes: A systematic review of the literature. *International Journal of Geriatric Psychiatry*, *28*(9), 914–924. https://doi.org/10.1002/gps.3913

Hackney, M. E., & Bennett, C. G. (2014). Dance therapy for individuals with Parkinson's disease: Improving quality of life. *Journal of Parkinsonism and Restless Legs Syndrome*, 4, 17–25.

Hall, J. M. (2018). Philosophy of dance and disability. *Philosophy Compass*, *13*(12), 1–10. https://doi.org/10.1111/phc3.12551

Hallal, P. C., Andersen, L. B., Bull, F. C., Guthold, R., & Haskell, W. (2012). Global physical activity levels: Surveillance progress, pitfalls, and prospects. *The Lancet*, *380*(9838), 247–257. https://doi.org/10.1016/S0140-6736(12)60646-1

Hanna, J. L. (2017). Dancing to resist, reduce, and escape stress. In V. Karkou, S. Oliver, & S. Lycouris (Eds.), *The Oxford handbook of dance and wellbeing* (pp. 99–114). Oxford University Press.

Hassall, H. (2023, September 17). *File on 4 (the dark side of ballet)* [Radio broadcast]. BBC. https://www.bbc.co.uk/programmes/m001qdt6

HCC. (2024). *Steady and strong dance class.* https://www.hants.gov.uk/socialcareandhealth/adultsocialcare/falls-prevention/danceclasses

Ho, R. T. H. et al. (2020). Psychophysiological effects of dance movement therapy and physical exercise on older adults with mild dementia: A randomized controlled trial. *The Journals of Gerontology*, *75*(3), 560–570. https://doi.org/10.1093/geronb/gby145

Hui, A. N. N., He, M. W. J., & Wong, W.-C. (2019). Understanding the development of creativity across the life span. In J. C. Kaufman & R. J. Stenberg (Eds.), *The Cambridge handbook of creativity* (pp. 69–86). Cambridge University Press.

ISTD. (2024). *Find your dance space*. Imperial Society of Teachers of Dancing. https://my.istd.org/findyourdancespace/

Jarrett, L. (2018, October/November). Stroke Odysseys: Performance arts after stroke, a service innovation for neurological rehabilitation. *British Journal of Neuroscience Nursing*, *14*, S18–S21. http://dx.doi.org/10.12968/bjnn.2018.14.Sup5.S18

Jarrett, L. (2024, February 20). Arts in health: What's changed in 25 years?. *Arts Professional*. Arts Professional Media. https://www.artsprofessional.co.uk/magazine/article/arts-health-whats-changed-25-years

Karkou, V., & Sanderson, P. (2000). Dance movement therapy in UK education. *Research in Dance Education*, *1*(1), 69–86. https://doi.org/10.1080/14647890050006596

Khan, H., & Giurca, B. et al. (2023). *Social prescribing around the world: A world map of global developments in social prescribing across different health system contexts*. National Academy for Social Prescribing. https://socialprescribingacademy.org.uk/media/4lbdy5ip/social-prescribing-around-the-world.pdf

Kim, S., & Kim, J. (2007). Mood after various brief exercise and sport modes: Aerobics, hip-hop dancing, ice skating, and body conditioning. *Perceptual and Motor Skills*, *104*, 1265–1270. https://doi.org/10.2466/pms.104.4.1265-1270

Koch, S. C., Riege, R. F. F., Tisborn, K., Biondo, J., Martin, L., & Beelmann, A. (2019). Effects of dance movement therapy and dance on health-related psychological outcomes. A meta-analysis update.

Frontiers in Psychology, *10*(1806), 1–28. https://doi.org/10.3389%2Ffpsyg.2019.01806

Kolb, A., & Haitzinger, N. (2023). 'Brexit put us in the Fridge, Covid in the Freezer': The impact of Covid-19 and Brexit on UK Freelance Dance. *Dance Research*, *41*(1), 40–65. https://doi.org/10.3366/drs.2023.0389

Kreutz, G., Bongard, S., Rohrmann, S., Hodapp, V., & Grebe, D. (2004). Effects of choir singing or listening on secretory immunoglobulin A, cortisol, and emotional state. *Journal of Behavioral Medicine*, *27*(6), 623–635. https://doi.org/10.1007/s10865-004-0006-9

Later Life Training. (2023). https://laterlifetraining.co.uk/dance-does-not-necessarily-reduce-falls-even-if-it-can-reduce-some-of-the-risk-factors-for-falls-review-of-evidence-from-the-older-people-and-frailty-policy-research-unit/

Leadbetter, C., & O'Connor, N. (2013). *Healthy attendance? The impact of cultural engagement and sports participation on health and satisfaction with life in Scotland*. Scottish Government Social Research. https://www.gov.scot/publications/healthy-attendance-impact-cultural-engagement-sports-participation-health-satisfaction-life-scotland/documents/

Liya, A., & Katoningsih, S. (2021). The development of learning the arts of dance to the ability of early childhood gross motor development. *Early Childhood Research Journal*, 4(2), 1–8.

Lopez-Nieves, I., & Jakobsche, C. E. (2022). Biomolecular effects of dance and dance/movement therapy: A review. *The American Journal of Dance Therapy*, *44*, 241–263. https://doi.org/10.1007/s10465-022-09368-z

Lovatt, P. (2020). *The dance cure*. Short Books Ltd.

Macmillan Cancer Support. (2013). *Cured – But at what cost?*. Macmillan Cancer Support. https://www.macmillan.org.uk/documents/cancerinfo/livingwithandaftercancer/consequences/cured-but-at-what-cost-report.pdf

Mansfield, L., Kay, T., Meads, C., Grigsby-Duffy, L., Lane, J., John, A., Daykin, N., Dolan, P., Testoni, S., Julier, G., Payne, A., Tomlinson, A., & Victor, C. (2018). Sport and dance interventions for healthy young people

(15-24 years) to promote subjective well-being: A systematic review. *BMJ Open*, *8*(7). https://doi.org/10.1136/bmjopen-2017-020959

Maraz, A., Király, O., Urbán, R., Griffiths, M., & Demetrovics, Z. (2015). Why do you dance? Development of the dance motivation inventory (DMI). *PLoS One*, *10*(3), 1–11. https://doi.org/10.1371/journal.pone.0122866

Marsh, K., & Whatley, S. (2017). *Making no difference: Inclusive dance pedagogy*. Routledge.

May, T., Chan, E. S., Lindor, E., McGinley, J., Skouteris, H., Austin, D., McGillivray, J., & Rinehart, N. J. (2021). Physical, cognitive, psychological and social effects of dance in children with disabilities: Systematic review and meta-analysis. *Disability and Rehabilitation*, *43*(1), 13–26. https://doi.org/10.1080/09638288.2019.1615139

Meehan, E., & Carter, B. (2021). Moving with pain: What principles from somatic practices can offer to people living with chronic pain. *Frontiers in Psychology*, *11*(620381), 1–10. https://doi.org/10.3389/fpsyg.2019.01806

Motta-Ochoa, R., Incio-Serra, N., Boulet, A., Fu, D., Frantz, A., William, M., & Blain-Moraes, S. (2021). Mouvement de passage: Creating connections through movement among persons with dementia. *Dementia*, *20*(7), 2573–2596. https://doi.org/10.1177/14713012211004009

National Academy for Social Prescribing. (2024). *Evidence on social prescribing*. National Academy for Social Prescribing. https://socialprescribingacademy.org.uk/read-the-evidence/

Neto, M. G., Menezes, M. A., & Carvalho, V. O. (2014). Dance therapy in patients with chronic heart failure: A systematic review and a meta-analysis. *Clinical Rehabilitation*, *28*(12), 1172–1179. https:/doi.org/10.1177/0269215514534089

NHS. (2014). *Building collaborative teams*. https://www.england.nhs.uk/improvement-hub/wp-content/uploads/sites/44/2019/01/Building-Collaborative-Teams-workshop-guide-2014-1.pdf

NHS. (2017). *Involving people in their own health and care: Statutory guidance for clinical commissioning groups and NHS England*. https://

www.england.nhs.uk/wp-content/uploads/2017/04/ppp-involving-people-health-care-guidance.pdf

NHS. (2019). *The long term plan*. https://www.longtermplan.nhs.uk/wp-content/uploads/2019/08/nhs-long-term-plan-version-1.2.pdf

Nietzsche, F. (1954). Thus spoke Zarathustra. In W. Kaufmann (Ed.), *The portable Nietzsche*. Penguin Books.

Noguera, C., Carmona, D., Rueda, A., Fernández, R., & Cimadevilla, J. M. (2020). Shall we dance? Dancing modulates executive functions and spatial memory. *International Journal of Environmental Research and Public Health*, *17*(1960), 1–17. https://doi.org/10.3390/ijerph17061960

Ocloo, J., Goodrich, J., Tanaka, H., Birchall-Searle, J., Dawson, D., & Farr, M. (2020). The importance of power, context and agency in improving patient experience through a patient and family centred care approach. *Health Research Policy and Systems*, *18*(10), 1–16. https://doi.org/10.1186/s12961-019-0487-1

O'Conner, K., Patterson-Price, J., & Faulkner, N. (2021). 'African Dance Is My Therapy': Perspectives on the unique health benefits of West African Dance. *Journal of Dance Education*, *21*(2), 72–81. https://doi.org/10.1080/15290824.2019.1678751

One Dance UK. (2023). *Considering difference – Making dance accessible*. One Dance UK. https://www.onedanceuk.org/resources/considering-difference-making-dance-accessible

ONS. (2022, December 6). *Cost of living and depression in adults, Great Britain: 29 September to 23 October 2022*. Office for National Statistics. https://www.ons.gov.uk/peoplepopulationandcommunity/healthandsocialcare/mentalhealth/articles/costoflivinganddepressioninadultsgreatbritain/29septemberto23october2022

Parmar, J. K., L'Hereux, T., Anderson, S., Duggleby, W., Pollard, C., Poole, L., Charles, L., Sonnenberg, L. K., Leslie, M., McGhan, G., Huhn, A., Sereda, S., Cecilia, M., Tarnowski, G., Mah, J., Melenberg, D., Weir, C., Pooler, C., … MacLachlan, N. (2022). Optimizing the integration of family caregivers in the delivery of person-centered care: Evaluation of an educational program for the healthcare workforce. *BMC Health Services Research*, *22*(364), 1–13. https://doi.org/10.1186/s12913-022-07689-w

Paxton, S. (2008). *The small dance*. https://myriadicity.net/contact-improv/learning-contact-improvisation/steve-paxtons-1977-small-dance-guidance

People Dancing. (2024). *Training and qualifications*. People Dancing. https://www.communitydance.org.uk/training-and-qualifications

Pereira-Stubbs, F. (2024). *Dance for health*. NHS Cambridge University Hospitals. https://www.cuh.nhs.uk/about-us/our-structure/other-departments/cuh-arts/our-programmes/live-and-participatory-arts/dance-for-health/

Petts, L., & Urmston, E. (2022). An exploration into the experience of family caregivers for people living with dementia in a community dance class. *Research in Dance Education*, *23*(1), 126–141. https://doi.org/10.1080/14647893.2021.1993175

Philip, K. E. J., Lewis, A., Williams, S., Buttery, S. C., Polkey, M. I., Man, W., Fancourt, D., & Hopkinson, N. S. (2020). Dance for people with chronic respiratory disease: A qualitative study. *BMJ Open*, *10*, 1–8. https://doi.org/10.1136/bmjopen-2020-038719

Pimsler, S. (2021). *The choreography of care: Engaging caregivers in creative expression*. HARP Publishing The People's Press.

Pontone, M., Vause, T., & Zonneveld, K. L. M. (2021). Benefits of recreational dance and behavior analysis for individuals with neurodevelopmental disorders: A literature review. *Behavioral Interventions*, *36*, 195–210. https://doi.org/10.1002/bin.1745

Powell, J. K., Costa, N., Schram, B., Hing, W., & Lewis, J. (2023). 'Restoring That Faith in My Shoulder': A qualitative investigation of how and why exercise therapy influenced the clinical outcomes of individuals with rotator cuff–related shoulder pain. *Physical Therapy*, *103*(12), 1–12. https://doi.org/10.1093/ptj/pzad088

Prieto, L. A., Haegele, J. A., & Columna, L. (2020). Dance programs for school-age individuals with disabilities: A systematic review. *Adapted Physical Activity Quarterly*, *37*(3), 349–376. https://doi.org/10.1123/apaq.2019-0117

Quin, E., Rafferty, S., & Tomlinson, C. (2015). *Safe dance practice. An applied dance science perspective*. Human Kinetics.

Quiroga, C. M., Bongard, S., & Kreutz, G. (2009). Emotional and neurohumoral responses to dancing tango Argentino: The effects of music and partner. *Music and Medicine*, *1*(1), 14–21. https://mmd.iammonline.com/index.php/musmed/article/view/MMD-2009-1-1-3

Ramachandran, V. S., & Seckel, E. L. (2011). Synchronized dance therapy to stimulate mirror neurons in autism. *Medical Hypotheses*, *76*, 150–151. https://doi.org/10.1016/j.mehy.2010.10.047

RCGP. (2021). *The power of relationships: What is relationship-based care and why is it important? General practice COVID-19 recovery*. https://www.rcgp.org.uk/getmedia/ca3e21e7-f742-47d7-9538-77e59bbb1ec7/power-of-relationships-rcgp-2021.pdf

Reason, M., & Reynolds, D. (2010). Kinesthesia, empathy and related pleasures: An inquiry into audience experiences of watching dance. *Dance Research Journal*, *42*(2), 49–75. https://doi.org/10.1017/S0149767700001030

Rebecchini, L. (2021). Music, mental health, and immunity. *Brain Behavior & Immunity – Health*, *18*, 100374. https://doi.org/10.1016/j.bbih.2021.100374

Rodley, I. (2020). *DAZL model and case study*. DAZL. http://dazl.org.uk/wp-content/uploads/2020/10/DAZL-Model-and-Case-Study-2020-Doc.pdf

Romaniuk, J. G., & Romaniuk, M. (1981). Creativity across the life span: A measurement perspective. *Human Development*, *24*(6), 366–381. https://doi.org/10.1159/000272732

Sanderson, P. (2008). The arts, social inclusion and social class: The case of dance. *British Educational Research Journal*, *34*, 467–490. https://doi.org/10.1080/01411920701609349

Sandman, L., Granger, B. B., Ekman, I., & Munthe, C. (2012). Adherence, shared decision-making and patient autonomy. *Medicine, Health Care, and Philosophy*, *15*(2), 115–127. https://doi.org/10.1007

Seppala, L., & Velde, N. (2022). How to tackle the global challenge of falls? *Age and Ageing*, *51*(11), 1–4. https://doi.org/10.1093/ageing/afac264

Skelton, D. (2010). *Effect of age, disease and inactivity on muscles function and balance related to risk of fall.* https://laterlifetraining.co.uk/wp-content/uploads/2010/08/EffectAgeBalance.pdf

Smith, A. (2013, May 7). 'Arts worth £5.9bn to UK economy' – Report. *The Stage.* https://www.thestage.co.uk/news/arts-worth-59bn-to-uk-economy-report

Smith, O. (2005). Shifting Apollo's frame: Challenging the body aesthetic in theater dance. In C. Sandahl & P. Auslander (Eds.) *Bodies in commotion: Disability and performance* (pp. 73–85). University of Michigan Press.

Smith, Z. (2018). The ageless quality of dance: Challenging perceptions of what people can achieve in later life. *Elder.* https://www.elder.org/the-elder/the-ageless-quality-of-dance-challenging-perceptions-of-what-people-can-achieve-in-later-life/

Sport England. (2023). *Active lives adults survey.* https://www.sportengland.org/media/13898/active-lives-adult-november-17-18-report.pdf

Stamp, K. (2022). How strictly is challenging the way people think about dance. *The Conversation.* https://theconversation.com/how-strictly-is-challenging-the-way-people-think-about-dance-192357.

Stevens, C., & McKechnie, S. (2005). Thinking in action: Thought made visible in contemporary dance. *Cognitive Processing*, 6(4), 243–252. https://doi.org/10.1007/s10339-005-0014-x

Stopgap Dance. (2024). *Inclusive choreography.* https://www.stopgapdance.com/inclusive-choreography/#translation

Stuart Pimsler Dance Theatre. (2023). *Arts & health.* http://www.stuartpimsler.com/arts-healthcare/

Swift, T. (2017). *Learning through movement and active play in the early years: A practical resource for professionals and teachers.* Jessica Kingsley Publishers.

Talker News. (2022). Why it's good for seniors to strut their stuff on the dance floor. *Talker.* https://talker.news/2022/11/04/why-its-good-for-seniors-to-strut-their-stuff-on-the-dance-floor/

Tammelin, T., Näyhä, S., Laitinen, J., Rintamäki, H., & Järvelin, M. (2003). Physical activity and social status in adolescence as predictors of physical inactivity in adulthood. *Preventive Medicine*, *37*(4), 375–381. https://doi.org/10.1016/s0091-7435(03)00162-2

Tao, D., Supriya, R., Gao, Y., Li, F., Liang, W., Jiao, J., Huang, W. Y., Dutheil, F., & Baker, J. S. (2021). Dementia and dance: Medication or movement?. *Physical Activity and Health*, *5*(1), 250–254. https://doi.org/10.5334/paah.138

Tarr, B., Launay, J., Cohen, E., & Dunbar, R. (2015). Synchrony and exertion during dance independently raise pain threshold and encourage social bonding. *Biology Letters*, *11*(10), 1–4. https://doi.org/10.1098/rsbl.2015.0767

Telama, R., Yang, X., Viikari, J., Välimäki, I., Wanne, O., & Raitakari, O. (2005). Physical activity from childhood to adulthood: A 21-year tracking study. *American Journal of Preventive Medicine*, *28*(3), 267–273. https://doi.org/10.1016/j.amepre.2004.12.003

The Neurological Alliance. (2022). *Together for the 1 in 6: UK Findings from My Neuro Survey*. The Neurological Alliance.

Tufnell, M. (2017). *When I open my eyes: Dance health imagination*. Dance Books Ltd.

Vahabi, M., & Damba, C. (2015). A feasibility study of a culturally and gender-specific dance to promote physical activity for South Asian immigrant women in the greater Toronto area. *Women's Health Issues: Official Publication of the Jacobs Institute of Women's Health*, *25*, 79–87. https://doi.org/10.1016/j.whi.2014.09.007

Vecchi, M., Elf, P., Ueno, A., Dilmperi, A., Dennis, C., & Devereux, L. (2022). Shall we dance? Recreational dance, well-being and productivity performance during COVID-19: A three-country study. *Journal of International Marketing*, *30*(2), 56–72. https://doi.org/10.1177/1069031X221079609. PMCID: PMC9133908.

Von Zimmermann, J., Vicary, S., Sperling, M., Orgs, G., & Richardson, D. C. (2018). The choreography of group affiliation. *Topics in Cognitive Science*, *10*(1), 1–5. https://doi.org/10.1111/tops.12320

Walker, P. (2021). *The miracle pill*. Simon & Schuster.

Weinstein, E. C., Clark, Z., DiBartolomeo, D. J., & Davis, K. (2014). A decline in creativity? It depends on the domain. *Creativity Research Journal*, *26*(2), 174–184. https://doi.org/10.1080/10400419.2014.901082

Whatley, S. (2007). Dance and disability: The dancer, the viewer and the presumption of difference. *Research in Dance Education*, *8*(1), 5–25. https://doi.org.10.1080/14647890701272639

Whatley, S. (2018). *Dance, disability and law: Invisible difference*. Intellect Books.

Whitehorse, L. E., Manzano, R., Baezconde-Garbanati, L. A., & Hahn, G. (1999). Culturally tailoring a physical activity program for Hispanic women: Recruitment successes of La Vida Buena's Salsa aerobics. *Journal of Health Education*, *30*, S18–S24. https://doi.org.10.1080/10556699.1999.10603424.

Whiteside, B. (2017). *Dance for Parkinson's Scotland (DfPS)*. https://scottish-ballet-assets.s3.amazonaws.com/uploads/2023/06/DfPS-Evaluation_B-Whiteside_July-2017-4.pdf

Whiteside, B. (2020). *Time to Dance: Exploring the Experiences of a Dementia-Friendly Programme*. https://scottish-ballet-assets.s3.amazonaws.com/uploads/2023/06/Time-to-Dance-Evaluation_Whiteside-2021-2.pdf

WHO. (2021, November 17). *Mental health of adolescents*. World Health Organisation. https://www.who.int/news-room/fact-sheets/detail/adolescent-mental-health

WHO. (2022a). *Self-care interventions for health*. World Health Organisation. https://www.who.int/health-topics/self-care#tab=tab_1

WHO. (2022b, October 1). *Aging and health*. World Health Organisation. https://www.who.int/news-room/fact-sheets/detail/ageing-and-health

WHO. (2022c, October 5). *Physical activity*. World Health Organisation. https://www.who.int/news-room/fact-sheets/detail/physical-activity

WHO. (2022d, December 1). *Long-term care*. World Health Organisation. https://www.who.int/europe/news-room/questions-and-answers/item/long-term-care

WHO. (2024, March 1). *Obesity and overweight*. World Health Organisation. https://www.who.int/news-room/fact-sheets/detail/obesity-and-overweight

Wicken, J. (2016). Count me in: Partnering with the arts to get the message out about inclusive WASH. *Water Aid*. https://washmatters.wateraid.org/blog/count-me-in-partnering-with-the-arts-to-get-the-message-out-about-inclusive-wash

Worthen-Chaudhari, L. (2011). New partnerships between dance and neuroscience: Embedding the arts for neurorecovery. *Dance Research*, 2, 469–496. https://doi.org/10.3366/drs.2011.0029

Youth Sport Trust. (2023). *Girls active national report*. Youth Sport Trust. https://www.youthsporttrust.org/research-listings/research/girls-active-national-reports

Zaporah, R. (1995). *Action theatre: The improvisation of presence*. North Atlantic Book.

ZoieLogic. (2021). *Fuzzy*. ZoieLogic Dance Theatre. https://zoielogic.co.uk/fuzzy/

INDEX

Printed in the USA
CPSIA information can be obtained
at www.ICGtesting.com
JSHW010008280924
70638JS00004B/6

9 781837 539154